Praise for *From Unknown*

G000060216

'If you're serious about getting more exposure for your ~~...~~ you as an industry leader, this is the book for you. By the end you'll have a rock-solid PR and social media strategy that you can immediately implement and raise your profile to expert status.'

Clinton Power, Founder, Blog Success School

'Catriona shows us HOW to write good copy and media releases, step by step. When you're given so many examples, it's easy to find one that relates to your own industry and use it for inspiration. This book is full of protein, not just fluff!'

Ken Burgin, CEO of Profitable Hospitality

'Catriona Pollard lays out a comprehensive and practical plan on how to build your profile and boost your personal brand.'

Valerie Khoo, journalist, Author of Power Stories

'Catriona articulates a clear path to building a reputation by using the art and craft of PR. In this refreshing book, not only has Catriona shared her wealth of experience and 'insiders secrets' to the world of PR, but she has also provided a step by step approach to build your authority. With a complete set of templates and examples, you can easily follow along – join the dots and get results for your career and your business.'

James Burgin, Creative Director, Brandwithin

'If you want to harness the power of public relations and social media to become a recognised expert in your field - this is the book you MUST buy!'

Andrew Griffiths, Australia's #1 small business and entrepreneurial author

'When you start building your personal brand strategically, amazing things happen. In From Unknown To Expert, Catriona holds our hand and walks us through the many aspects of successfully establishing our authority and finding our voice so that we can effectively share our knowledge and our gifts with others. I recommend you read and take action.'

Suzi Dafnis, Community Director & CEO, Australian Business Women's Network

From Unknown To Expert

How to Use Clever PR and Social Media to Become a Recognised Expert

Catriona Pollard

First published in 2014 by GreenTara
Suite 404, 10-12 Clarke St
Crows Nest NSW 2065

National Library of Australia Cataloguing in Publications data:
Author: Catriona Pollard
Title: From Unknown to Expert: How to Use Clever PR and Social Media to Become a Recognised Expert
ISBN: 978-0-646-92142-6
Subject: Business, Entrepreneurship

To Warren, Denise, Jo, Charlie and Sarah.

Contents

How to use this book

STAR 1 Figuring out the why   1

The importance of you and PR   2

My story (well, one of them!)   4

Unknown To Expert 5 Star System   9

The start of your story   10

STAR 2 Setting the stage   12

Personal brand   14

Elevator statement   15

Key messages   18

Your bio   21

Target audiences   26

STAR 3 Turn on the spotlight   28

Your personal website   30

Create your own blog   32

Guest blogging   41

Networking   45

Stepping on stage   46

STAR 4 Use the media to shine the light   64

Getting the media interested   66

Dealing with the media   72

Tactic 1: Media releases   75

Tactic 2: The perfect pitch   84

Tactic 3: Contributed articles   96

Features lists   101

Media lists   106

Following up the media   110

Media interviews   114

Blogger outreach   117

STAR 5 Own the light   **121**

Planning social   123

Managing your time on social media   126

What social media platforms are right for you?   128

Facebook   130

LinkedIn   137

Twitter   146

YouTube   150

Google+   154

Instagram   156

Pinterest   158

The beginning   161

Get inspired with Catriona Pollard   164

How to use this book

By the end of this book the goal is for you to move from unknown to recognised expert by using clever PR and social media tactics and strategies.

You should finish with a complete strategic PR and social media plan to help skyrocket you and your role as a thought leader into the spotlight.

Depending on what stage you are at in moving from unknown to expert you can use this book in a few ways. It also depends on how you learn.

As a step-by-step 'activity program'

Start from the beginning and work right through to the end:

1. Read through each section which are building blocks for your PR and social media strategy.
2. Complete each Action Step as you go through the process as they will assist you in applying what you are learning.

The benefit of using the book in this particular way is it provides you with a complete set of tools, strategies and tactics to create and maintain your profile as an expert and thought leader.

Dipping in and out

This book can be used on an ad-hoc basis, meaning you can 'dip in and out' of sections and chapters. This flexibility has been created as not every person is at the same skill level and may be at different stages of building their profile as an expert and thought leader.

Read and come back

You can read through the book and then come back to the Action Steps. Please do come back to the steps as they are designed to assist in applying the skills I've covered in the book.

However you choose to use this program, I believe you will finish with a sound and valuable knowledge base of tactics that will serve you well in creating a successful and profitable PR and social media campaign for your role as an expert and thought leader.

BONUS Action Steps - No matter what, take action

Throughout this book you will see I've included relevant and interactive Action Steps for you to take so that you can immediately start to gain some traction towards your goal of becoming a highly sought after expert.

There are **32 Bonus Action Steps** available to you as you work your way through this book.

You can access and download these interactive Action Step Files by visiting:
www.UnknownToExpertBonus.com

These Action Steps are absolutely key to you becoming a recognised expert.

You can be sure that other experts at the top of your industry have taken, and still are taking, significant action towards growing their profile as a thought leader.

In other forums you might pay hundreds or even thousands of dollars for these Action Steps.

As a special bonus to you, as a reader of this book, they're yours for free as my gift.

So please, make sure you do them!

Taking action

No matter how you choose to use this information, without action you will achieve very little.

It can be a difficult process moving from unknown to expert. At times you may feel overwhelmed with the amount of work you need to do, and the volume of learning opportunities in this program.

I urge you to move beyond feeling overwhelmed and into action.

Transforming from unknown to expert takes patience, practice and focus. If you do get distracted, overwhelmed, or if it never leaves the 'to do list', ask the question, why?

Why do you want to move from unknown to expert? What is your motivation?

Write yourself a note, add it as your screen saver, or stick it on the wall in your office. Read it every time you feel stuck.

I believe in you. I know the world will be a better place with more people sharing their ideas, opinions and expertise. **TAKE ACTION**.

Figuring out the why?

The importance of you and PR

Public relations and social media can be the difference between being a well recognised expert and thought leader in your niche, and just wishing you were.

Public relations is the art of storytelling. Every person, brand and organisation has stories tell and amazing stories deserves audiences.

Our stories can be personal stories, professional stories, stories that let people know who we are, what we stand for, what we do.

And when we start telling our stories, they start resonating with people. Those people start developing relationships with us and start influencing and amplifying your role as an expert and thought leader.

But what's in it for you?

Public relations and social media enhances your profile, reputation and credibility.

When you are well recognised as an expert in your field, your target audience, key organisations and the media take notice of you.

And you know what happens when people take notice of you? Increased sales, more paid speaking opportunities, more referrals, doors start opening and new opportunities you never even dreamed of start falling into your lap.

How does it work?

Every expert has so many stories to tell that will interest influencers and the media.

The trick is to identify your stories and then see them through the eyes of the editors and program directors. When packaged in a way that the media expects, you have a much better chance of getting the media coverage you need to promote yourself.

Anything from an innovation, new book, to a childhood memory has news potential if it's packaged correctly. And it has absolutely no news value if it isn't released to the media or shared online at all!

This book will give you all the tools and knowledge you need to help you develop your PR and social media skills and successfully achieve the role as a recognised expert and thought leader.

My story (well, one of them!)

We all have stories to tell. This is one of mine.

I tossed and turned in my bed, unable to sleep. I had moments where I was on the precipice of panic. It was 8 November 2010, and the next evening I had to walk on stage and present to 100 people on how to use PR and social media.

So filled with panic and anxiety, I had gone to the venue in the afternoon so I could practice on the stage. I thought: "If I can just get up on stage before everyone is there, I'll be able to imagine myself presenting to the audience. I'll be able to manage my nerves".

It made it worse.

I ended up in tears, wanting to cancel the whole thing. Now I was even more nervous and deeply believed I couldn't do it. I just didn't know how I was going to manage my nerves and I wondered if the audience would think I didn't know enough about PR and social media.

Months before this night, I had known I wanted to put myself into this challenging position. I wanted to change a theme of my life.

I am an introvert. I've always been unwilling to be in the spotlight. Public speaking was one of the biggest issues I had never been able to overcome.

My sister gets up in front of people for a living; she is a corporate trainer. One time she booked me into a presentation skills course through her work. I lasted about 10 minutes, dashing from the room in tears, leaving my sister to go and rescue my handbag and put me in a taxi.

That was just one time. There have been countless situations throughout my life which I ran away from or said no to because I had to stand in the spotlight: school head prefect, job promotions, speaking at conferences… so many. It was a theme in my life. And it was time to change it.

9 November 2010, 6:30pm was a pivotal moment in my personal history.

At 6:00pm the room started filling up. People were walking into the room full of expectation, wanting to learn about PR and social media. They came to hear me speak, to learn from me.

I knew some of the people in the audience. Many came because they knew of me through social media and wanted to hear my presentation. I felt an enormous pressure to perform.

I looked at my watch. It was 6:25pm. Do I run or do I stay? I knew it was time to change the theme. But could I do it?

At 6:30pm I walked up the stairs with the microphone in my hand, trying to not let my hand shake. I walked across the darkened stage and... into the spotlight.

I looked at the light shining from the spotlight. There was absolute silence as the audience waited. I looked out to the crowd. I took a breath and I began to speak.

And do you know what happened?

I realised that I deserved to be in this very spotlight. I wanted people to hear me speak.

I wanted a voice that would carry across the room into the hearts and minds of the audience.

Do you know why?

Because I had something to say. I had so many things to say.

What I had to say could change their business, could help them get more customers, build relationships with interesting people and help them build their profile. What I had to say could do so many wonderful things for so many people.

Who was I *not* to stand in the spotlight? Who was I *not* to share expert information? Who was I *not* to have a voice? Who was I *not* to be a shining star?

And so I opened my mouth and the words and sentences were perfectly formed. It was the start of my journey to becoming a well-recognised and highly regarded expert and thought leader.

Within just 12 months of that first nervous and exciting step into the spotlight, everything changed.

I now get asked to speak internationally. (Seriously! I can't believe it myself sometimes). I have received millions of dollars worth of media coverage, I'm listed in the top 100 PR people to follow on Twitter, have an award winning blog and am placed in the Top 5% of people using social media.

How it all started

As a PR professional I spent over 20 years putting other people in the spotlight, and didn't even think about myself being there.

But I got sick of saying no. I wanted to change a theme in my life. I wanted to say yes to more 'spotlight' opportunities.

So I made a clear decision to start building my profile as an expert and thought leader. I intuitively knew it was my time to step into the spotlight.

I have to tell you it wasn't easy for me. So let me share with you what I found, so it's easier for you.

My suggestion to you before you start on your journey is to do two things:

1. Stand in your power.
2. Explore your motivation about why you want to develop your profile.

1. Stand in your power

The first thing to do before starting to build your profile is to stand in your power. Before I started my thought leadership journey I had self-limiting beliefs about telling my story:

- Did I know enough?
- What if I get up on stage and forget everything?
- Do I know more than the next PR person?
- Am I really an expert?

I had to back myself, believe in myself, and stand in my own power.

I had to believe that I am truly an expert, and be prepared to tell people I was.

And so do you.

2. Explore your motivation

The second element is to explore your motivation. What is your motivation to build your profile as an expert and thought leader? If the only reason you are doing it is to get more sales, your audience will know that. And they won't like it.

After my pivotal moment on 9 November 2010 I realised it was bigger than overcoming a challenge. It wasn't about me. It was about you.

My motivation was to create new opportunities and business growth, but more deeply it was to share my knowledge. It was to teach as many people as I could about how to do amazing PR and social media.

It's taken a few years. Within 12 months I achieved 43 pieces of media coverage in outlets such as Australian Financial Review, BRW, CEO Online, Sydney Morning Herald, PR Week US, Management Today and many others. I spoke to hundreds of people and really started getting traction with my profile.

In the second year I achieved 146 pieces of media coverage, landed the account for Hilton Worldwide across Australia and New Zealand without even a competitive pitch. (They read my blog, saw the work we did through our media coverage and asked for a meeting).

By the end of the year I had cemented myself as an expert in PR and social media, with regular columns in some of Australia's widely read business publications including CEO Online, LeadingCompany and Marketing Magazine. I was the social media go-to-person for SmartCompany and Sydney Morning Herald small business section. I was consistently getting paid for speaking and work was flowing in.

How I did it (and how you can too)

So, even though I had a lot of PR and social media experience putting other people in the spotlight, going through the process of becoming a recognised expert myself really enabled me to clarify the key steps in the process and I was able to distil it down to five steps.

I call it the Unknown To Expert 5 Star System.

I have consistently used my Unknown To Expert 5 Star System with a clear intent to build my profile, and it's worked every time. It can work for you too. Because it's a proven, reliable, repeatable formula for going From Unknown To Expert.

What I'm doing in this book is sharing with you how this system works. How I did it, and how I've done it for thousands of other experts and thought leaders.

Now it's your time to stand in the spotlight.

Unknown To Expert 5 Star System

This book takes you through the Unknown To Expert 5 Star System. A system I developed on my path from unknown to expert and I'm so excited to share it with you.

The Unknown To Expert 5 Star System illuminates your path to success.

When you are unknown, you are in the darkness. Your light is not shining and your stories are not being told. You may be an expert, but you are not making the world a better place by proactively sharing your ideas, opinions and expertise.

The Unknown To Expert 5 Star System is a pathway that moves you from darkness to a star that people see. They take notice of you. You are illuminated.

You become recognised as an expert and thought leader. You are known, liked, respected and trusted.

When you have completed the Unknown To Expert 5 Star System you will have increased sales, more paid speaking opportunities, more referrals and new opportunities.

I developed this system on my path from unknown to expert. It worked for me, it can work for you.

The start of your story

Often we think we have to be amazing experts to even talk or write about a topic.

Sometimes the title 'expert' doesn't sit quite right. It might feel as though everybody's an expert these days. But the truth is, you have knowledge in your particular field that others don't, and you can capitalise on this by offering your expert comments and opinion to the media and on social media.

The more you accept that you are an expert, the more everybody else will accept it too.

The more that you use PR and social media to put yourself forward as the expert, the more credible your own profile becomes.

The more people who know about you, the more chances you have of landing a new business opportunity or promotion.

Reputation is the new currency – particularly in social media – and we want a bucket load of it to work effectively for you. It's also about trust; people do business with people and brands they trust.

When you become a known expert, it is your name and job title that is published for people in your industry and the general public to see. This helps with your credibility, and journalists will start calling you when they need an expert.

In social media, it's about referrals and connections. So when you start building your online reputation by writing guest articles on blogs, offering amazing free content, sharing interesting links and interacting with people, soon you'll hear yourself being talked about - "she knows her stuff", "he's very authentic" or "I would recommend her".

If you are applying for a board position or new job, it makes sense that if you are featured in the media or have a great social media profile, you will have an increased chance of landing the position, compared to the person who isn't.

With a high profile, people will believe that you are an expert; they will trust you, and your reputation will start to open doors. And that's what you get out of building your profile.

But what do others get out of it?

This is what I believe we need to really think about before we embark on building our own profile and reputation.

I believe we all have stories to tell that will help others in some way. We have experience and expertise we have developed along the way that should be shared because others will benefit from it.

So when you are thinking about building your profile, come at it from the perspective of how you can help others. It's totally fine that you are doing it for your own gain. Of course, it's an essential element to building your career and business!

But if it's purely promotional, you won't develop the emotional connections with people in the same way as if you are doing it from your authentic self.

When you start telling your stories and sharing your expertise because it is helping the people who are listening or reading it, you will be amazed with the emotional connection that you start building with people and the relationships you start developing – because you're positively impacting their lives.

Your Motivation

Really take the time to start exploring your motivation about why you want to develop your profile. You'll be coming back to it for inspiration as you go through moving from unknown to recognised expert. Open your Action Step and start now.

Visit **www.UnknownToExpertBonus.com**
For Your FREE Bonus Action Step Content

ACTION STEP

1

Setting the Stage

At Star 2, you are setting the stage, working out your personal brand, your elevator statement and what you want people to know about you.

Remember that thought leadership is more than writing a couple of articles or doing a few speaking gigs. It's truly leading a space and serving as a resource for others in your area.

This section is your chance to set the foundations of your PR and social media strategy, so you can start to build a genuine and long-lasting role as a thought leader.

It will guide you through the basics which you can build on throughout the next sections.

Setting the foundations is all about planning what you want to be known as an expert in, and how you are going to articulate it.

It's about you and your brand, who you want to be targeting, what you will need to do in order to create your media angles and pitches for the media, and where you will be pitching these angles.

At the end of this section you will have a clear idea about who you are, how to express your brand, and who will help you skyrocket your role as expert.

Personal brand

Personal branding is how you market yourself to others. Your personal brand is what people say about you when you're not around. It's what you're known for.

You need to be intentional about creating your brand, or others will create it for you.

Do some thinking about who you are, what you stand for, what value you offer.

Have a think about the heart and soul of your brand – your 'one thing'. This is the essence of your communication and the voice of your strategy across every platform.

For example, if Disney = magic, Apple = innovation, Richard Branson = entrepreneurship, Layne Beachley = determination – what is your one thing? Mine is inspiration.

Do you want to be "professional", "humorous", "hard working", "affordable", "high end", "ethical"?

At this stage it's also important to think about your area of expertise. What is your niche? What are you an expert and thought leader in?

It's critical that you pick your niche and stick to it. Don't be wishy-washy as it will confuse your audience and dilute your brand.

Clearly, my niche is public relations and social media. Everything I do comes back to this platform. I don't talk about business planning, or write articles about marketing – only about PR and social media.

Your Personal Brand

What is your one thing?
Jump to the Action Step and start your personal branding process.

Visit **www.UnknownToExpertBonus.com**
For Your FREE Bonus Action Step Content

Elevator statement

So what do you do? Can you easily answer that question?

An elevator statement or pitch is a quick summary that you use in any situation where you need to explain your role as a thought leader and what you do in a clear and concise manner.

It's called an 'elevator statement' because you should be able to get through your whole speech in the time it takes to travel from the ground floor to the top floor in an elevator (10-30 seconds).

An elevator statement can help promote you and leave a great first impression. You want people to remember who you are and what you are an expert in. This could help you gain new customers, speaking opportunities or media interviews. It also means you are helping them 'talk about you' and share your personal brand.

Qualities of a good elevator statement

A good elevator statement does several things:
* It captures the listener's attention.
* It explains the 'what' and 'why' simply and clearly.
* It ends with a call to action.

How to create an elevator statement

Identify your objectives

What is the point of your elevator statement? Identify your objectives and incorporate them into your statement. Your elevator statement will be more successful if it helps you to achieve your goal. You might need to create a few different statements if you have different goals.

Develop action statements

Create statements or questions designed to motivate another person to help you achieve your objective. For example if your objective is to get a deal with a publisher for a book, then include a statement in your pitch that will let the person you are speaking with know your goal is to be a published author.

Record yourself

Listening to a recording of yourself can help you to critique your performance and improve it. You can also determine which pitch or approach is the best.

Get another opinion

Once you have perfected your pitch to fit into a 10-30 second time frame, present it to another person to gain their feedback. You should choose someone who you trust and who already has an understanding of what you do, such as colleagues, clients, friends and family. You can then gain the most appropriate feedback.

Practice

Now you have your final product. Write it down and memorise it so you are comfortable delivering it in any situation.

Update it

There is always room for improvement. Listen to how other people introduce themselves and pick up phrases that you thought were effective. Continually update your elevator statement when your business or position changes.

An elevator statement is an important marketing tool for yourself and your business that can help you gain new customers and clients.

Here are some examples of elevator statements:

- I use public relations and social media tools to help businesses and people achieve their dreams. Catriona Pollard
- I design and produce a range of vibrational gemstone jewellery that is beautiful and spiritual. I often joke it is for closet spiritual people because you can wear it from the boardroom, to the market, to the yoga mat. Eilish Bouchier

- Parenting Fun Everyday is 'creating family fun for everyone, every single day of the year through craft, food, celebrations, travel, and nurturing'. Amber Schmida Greene
- I help people reduce pain and stress by gently activating their body's self-healing capacity resulting in long-lasting change. www.brucestark.com.au
- You know the feeling when you think about your last holiday, and a smile spreads over your face? Well, that's Journey Jottings. We help you highlight your holiday adventures so the fun in those memories will still be putting a smile on your face in 10 years' time. Linda Fairbairn
- I help energised entrepreneurs create opt-in strategies that bring in red hot leads daily. www.betterbusinessbetterlife.com.au

Your Elevator Statement

3

ACTION STEP

Now it's time to develop your own elevator statement. Open your Action Step and start now.

Visit **www.UnknownToExpertBonus.com**
For Your FREE Bonus Action Step Content

Key messages

The next step after creating your elevator statement is to draft your key messages. In PR we use key messages in everything, from preparing for a media interview, through to writing copy for websites and brochures. But what are they?

Key messages are the core messages you want your target audience to hear and remember. They are what you must say and get across when communicating with your target audience, particularly in a media interview. These points are really important because they allow you to deliver consistent communication and create a uniform perception of your brand in the marketplace.

Key messages are an extension of the elevator statement. They add depth and meaning to the work you do and your position as an expert. You should have around five key messages which answer the following criteria:

- Believable: They are supported with evidence.
- Easy to understand: They reflect your target audience's understanding, needs and wants.
- Distinctive: They establish what makes you stand out from the crowd.
- Purposeful: They drive your agenda.
- Positive: They use positive language.
- Digestible: They are short, concise and to the point.

Developing your key messages

When developing your key messages, consider the following:

1. **Amount:** You should aim for around five key messages. These messages are made up of only the most important pieces of information, so the more concise the better.
2. **Who do you target?** Consider your target audiences. What do they need and want to hear from you? Do you have multiple target

audiences? If so, ensure you tailor your target messages to each individual market.

3. **Keep it simple:** A good key message is simple and to the point. Over-complicating your messages will just lead to confusion and will often cause more harm than good.

4. **Review:** Over time your messages will have to slowly change and evolve – nothing stays the same forever. Review and update your messages regularly to ensure you do not communicate old news and values.

Individual example:

- Jane Smith provides expert financial advice in the areas of accounting, business advisory, wealth accumulation and investment planning to help individuals and businesses thrive.
- Jane Smith is an expert in financial planning with 20 years in the industry, providing financial advice to organisations such as Company X, Company Y and Company Z.
- Jane Smith provides a unique process that is simple, yet effective in forming a structured plan that will help maximise the client's future financial security.
- Jane Smith is a recognised thought leader who shares her finance expertise as a media commentator and regular contributor to AFR, BRW and Sky News.

Business example:

- Company X is a leading content agency that creates strategic and custom content for brands across any channel or platform, including print, video, digital, gaming and broadcast.
- The Company X team is a pioneer in content marketing in Australia, innovatively using multiple forms of communication to deliver creative and results-driven campaigns.
- Company X works closely with brands to develop creative

content campaigns that engage audiences and deliver specific business outcomes, such as increased sales, loyalty and customer satisfaction.

- Company X adopts a strategic approach to content marketing to help clients make the most of their content assets.
- The Company X team includes industry experts with international best-practice experience. They include Person A, Person B and Person C.

Your Key Messages

What are your key messages?
How do you want people to remember you?
Jump over to the Action Step page and develop your own key messages.

Visit **www.UnknownToExpertBonus.com**
For Your FREE Bonus Action Step Content

Your bio

As an expert, you need to become adept in the art of selling yourself to your target audience, to the media and to conference organisers.

It is useful to have an up-to-date bio on hand to share with event organisers when pitching yourself as a speaker, with publications looking to publish an article you have written or with journalists looking to learn more about you. You should also include your bio on your website.

An expert bio is just one tool you will use to prove you are qualified and experienced. It plays a critical role, as it communicates and demonstrates your role as a thought leader. It serves as a short introduction to who you are and what you're an expert in – it's the basis of what you want people to think of when they hear your name.

An expert bio is not simply a resume. It should describe and showcase your career, highlight the topics or fields that you are an expert in, and sell you in a genuine way.

How to write an expert bio

Step one: Planning your bio

Sell yourself, but not in a slimy way

You are the brand and your thought leadership is your product, so write about yourself in a way that is active, attractive and genuine. The reader needs to be hooked and enticed to keep reading. Write your bio in the third person.

Use the inverted pyramid method

No, this isn't a maths equation! It's a method we use in PR where we add the most important information at the start and the least important information at the end. Most of us are lazy readers. We tend to only read the first few paragraphs, so you want your readers to recognise you're an expert quickly.

Create multiple versions: Long, short, micro

Create a few versions of your bio for certain situations – you may need a short bio (100 words) to send through to a journalist, or a longer bio (one page) to send to a conference organiser, or a really short one (one or two sentences) to add to the bottom of an article, or Twitter profile.

Keep it up to date

Be ruthless with your draft copies until you are 100 percent happy with the finished product. Add a reminder to your diary to go back to your bio every couple of months, as you may have achieved a book deal or media coverage that you want to add.

Make it easy for people to contact you

Always include contact information (even if it's just a website on your micro version).

Consider your audience

Think about where you will use your bio – you might be sending this to the media, business associates and conference organisers. Take some time to think about your readers, what is it they need to know about you? How can you help them form opinions about you quickly? Don't be afraid to tailor your bio for specific audiences.

Step two: Writing your bio

Now start adding some detail

- Your name and job title or role
- Your area of expertise
- Your background and experience
- Examples to demonstrate you as a thought leader i.e. media coverage, speaking roles, publications or articles you have written.
- Your qualifications
- Add an image (optional)

Examples

Ros Moriarty, Managing Director and co-founder of the Jumbana Group

Micro:

MD Jumbana P/L Indigenous design & strategy and author of Listening to Country. Co-founder, co-chair non-profit Nangala Project. *jumbana. com.au*

Long:

Ros Moriarty is Managing Director and co-founder of the Jumbana Group, and creative director of Balarinji Studio. Established in 1983, the Jumbana Group is a national and international trailblazer in communications and Indigenous strategy in the resource, infrastructure, tourism, media and sport sectors. Ros has established, driven and maintained a profitable and high profile business for almost three decades. She is also the co-founder and chair of the DGR non-profit Nangala Project.

Born in Tasmania, Ros is a graduate of the Australian National University, and was formerly a journalist with Radio Australia in Indigenous affairs, women's issues and the environment. She has also held senior positions with the Federal Department of Aboriginal Affairs in Canberra and Sydney, and Australian Volunteers Abroad.

Ros' Board appointments have included the Council of the National Gallery of Australia, Australian Major Events, the Council of the Australian Academy of Design, and the Board of the Menzies School of Health Research, Darwin.

She has been awarded South Australian Business Woman of the Year, the Advance Australia Award for Service to Industry and Commerce, and the St Peter's Citizenship Award. She was inducted into the Australian Business Women's Hall of Fame in 1999, and the same year was a finalist in the NSW Telstra Business Women's Awards.

Ros' memoir, Listening to Country, was published by Allen & Unwin in 2010, was shortlisted for The Age Book of the Year 2010, was a Finalist in the Australian Human Rights Commission Literary Awards, and won the National Year of Reading 2012 Awards, Northern Territory.

Fergus Stoddart – Commercial Director, Edge

Long:

As a founder of Edge, Fergus has spent nine years devising and launching customer engagement strategies for their portfolio of blue chip clients.

With a commercial and publishing background, Fergus specialises in developing the commercial opportunities behind each project and leveraging the media that each database presents. Initially as publisher focusing on building revenue from the cruise publishing portfolio from a single title, to a suite of consumer and custom publishing products to running the advertising sales function.

He oversaw the growth of custom advertising revenue from $2m to $5m. Fergus now focuses on developing customer engagement strategies for new clients from conception to early execution. He also creates the commercial strategy for each new launch.

Over the years as the Director responsible for new business development, Fergus has been responsible for winning major blue chip accounts for Edge including Woolworths, BMW, VW, Crown Casino and Carnival Australia.

Fergus began his career in the family business and a graduate training role at Coke before moving to Australia to pursue an MBA at Macquarie University, after which he founded Edge.

Mark Gabbott, Executive Dean of Macquarie University's Faculty of Business and Economics

Short:

Professor Mark Gabbott is Executive Dean of Macquarie University's Faculty of Business and Economics. His current research interests are in services marketing, knowledge management, customer relationship management, consumer behaviour and customer value. Mark has published four books, his research has been published in a variety of academic journals and he sits on the editorial boards of three international marketing journals.

Your Bio

Now it's time to create your bio.
Jump over to the Action Step page to create micro,
short and long versions of your expert bio.

Visit **www.UnknownToExpertBonus.com**
For Your FREE Bonus Action Step Content

Target audiences

If PR stands for public relations, it stands to reason that a vital part of PR is determining who your public is – that is, your target audiences.

Your target audiences come down to who you want to build your profile as an expert and thought leader with. Think about your target audiences based on their profession, industry, geography, interests and age.

In order to define your target audiences, focus on these elements:

Type of profession and title

Who are the influencers and decision makers? Think about their title i.e. CEO, HR Director, CIO.

Type of industries

For example, if your area of expertise is leadership and career development then you would look to target people in business and HR, but you could also target business leaders and HR Managers across industries such as finance, SMEs, corporate, IT, banking, franchising, hospitality or education.

The specific industries you target will depend on your target audiences. If you are targeting financial planners who own their own business, then your target industries would include finance, business, SMEs and HR.

Geographic area

Want to be a global expert? Then you need to think global, beyond just your local town or country. Alternatively, if you want to build your influence in your local community, then all you need to do is start getting local media coverage and building relationships with local influencers.

Area of interest

What is your area of interest? For example, if you are a crafter that wants to build your profile as an expert in macramé then you would focus on craft, art, interior design and macramé influencers.

What is their age?

If you have a product that is aimed at teenagers, have a think about where they get their information from. Think about online as well as print, such as magazines.

Gender

Are you targeting men or women, or both? Who has the most influence on your personal brand and your reputation as a thought leader?

Clearly defining your target audiences will help you get the best results because your efforts will be targeted to the people who will help you move from unknown to expert.

Your Target Audience

Who are your target audiences? Clarify your target audiences. Open your Action Step and start now.

Visit **www.UnknownToExpertBonus.com**
For Your FREE Bonus Action Step Content

Turn on the Spotlight

At Star 3 you're starting to shine. You are getting your personal website done, starting to create networks around your brand, and stepping on stage.

Now you have done your planning and have your elevator statement, key messages, bio and target audiences, it's time to turn on the spotlight and illuminate your role as an expert and thought leader.

This section will help you start to spread your messages and stand in the spotlight through a personal website and blog. It will show you how to use other blogs to position yourself, and how to meet other people at networking functions and use your elevator statement.

This section also covers how to develop your speaker's profile and start getting speaking opportunities.

At the end of this section you will be on the path to becoming a recognised expert by starting to build awareness about you.

Your personal website

A personal website gives you an online platform where you can promote yourself, be easily found and can act as the central hub for all of your information and social media links.

It means you can 'own' your information and it will give you more control over your online identity. You'll be more easily found online by your target audiences, journalists and event organisers.

Features to include on your personal website:

- **Expert's biography** – This is where you can share your passions and your expertise.
- **Your credentials** – This is your elevator statement, i.e. a brief statement explaining why people should listen to you and what makes you an expert in the subject matter.
- **A blog** – Regularly adding your expertise in a blog format will assist in building your profile as a thought leader and expert. This is covered in more detail later in this chapter.
- **Speaker's profile** – If you plan on speaking, add your speaker's profile to your website (covered in this chapter).
- **Social media channels** – add your links and feeds to your site.
- **Testimonials** – These can be testimonials of your expertise in the subject matter, speaking and consulting.
- **Images** – A professional photo and images of you speaking etc
- **Media coverage** – Include links to any online media coverage you have received. Do not include copies of print media coverage as this can breach copyright.
- **Contact details** – phone number, email, social media links.

Name it!

Your personal website ideally includes your name in the URL. For example, www.janesmith.com. The first step is to buy your own URL from sites such as Go Daddy or Netregistry. It's easy to do, and domain names are priced from around $10 per year.

Choose your format

You can create your personal website using a website format with the home page relatively static and one of the pages as a blog. Alternatively, you can build it in a blog format so your home page is your blog and your pages include your bio, speakers profile etc.

For example:

Website format: www.SocialMediaSydney.com.au

Blog format: www.PublicRelationsSydney.com.au

One of the easiest platforms to use is Wordpress.

You can set up a site at www.wordpress.org. It uses open-sourced software and has a great range of design templates and add-ons such as plug-ins for your site.

When selecting your website design, you can access Wordpress' free templates, or if you prefer, you can customise your design with one of the inexpensive themes available for Wordpress.

You can also pay to have a customised design created by a web designer. This is a little more time consuming, but it's worth the effort so your website reflects your brand.

You will need to buy your URL and find your own web host such as www.netregistry.com.au or www.BlueHost.com.

You don't need to be a technical whiz. It does take a little time to do the initial set up, but once you have done that all you need is your ideas for the site and away you go.

Your Personal Website

Can you visualise your personal website?
Now is the time to work through what it will look like and the types of information it will contain.
Open your Action Step and start taking action!

Visit **www.UnknownToExpertBonus.com**
For Your FREE Bonus Action Step Content

ACTION STEP 7

Create your own blog

As you are turning up the spotlight to illuminate your role as a thought leader, it's essential to use blogging as a tool to increase your profile and reputation.

In my opinion, blogs are the best way of demonstrating your expertise online, controlling your message and building your reputation.

Blogs are a fluid, dynamic medium, more akin to a 'conversation'.

The power of a blog is that when you are blogging, you are a journalist. When you use PR tactics such as pitching stories to the media, you need to convince them your story is interesting. However, when you have your own blog, you can publish anything you think is interesting and relevant.

Not only do you have control over what is published, you own the copyright to it.

Blogs allow you to easily publish your ideas, readers can interact with you and you can build relationships with them.

Blogging allows you to differentiate yourself from your competitors, showcase your personality, share information about yourself, team or company.

The benefits of blogging

- Builds your profile through demonstrating expertise.
- Allows you to share information and build relationships with clients/customers.
- Informs people about other things you are doing such as speaking at events or commenting in the media.
- Generates powerful referral networks.
- Creates an opportunity to network and share information with people globally.
- Improves your ranking on search engines.

Planning

Before you set up your blog, do some research and take a look at blogs in your area of expertise, blogs you've read before and blogs you currently read. Look up your competitors' blogs and people you admire in your industry.

I think this is a good idea, even if you have already set up your blog. I regularly read blogs in my area of expertise (as well as many not in my area!) – that's how I learn what other people are doing. It provides inspiration for your blog.

Creating Your Blog

Take the time to do some blog planning; it will really clarify your ideas and thoughts.
Open the Action Step and start jotting down your ideas.

Visit **www.UnknownToExpertBonus.com**
For Your FREE Bonus Action Step Content

Types of blog posts

One way to remain creative and relevant when writing your blog is to use different blog post formats.

How to/tutorial posts

A 'how to' post is meant to educate your readers and give them practical information about a topic, a task or an issue. It's your chance to share your expertise and to prove your credentials by giving back value.

Example: How to become a confident public speaker.

List posts

List posts go through a number of tips, hints, strategies and tactics that help the readers. List posts are similar to how-to posts but their format means they are used as steps to achieve a goal rather than guides.

Example: Five ways to use Facebook to market your product.

Case studies

As a business person and an expert in your field you may be able to share case studies that illustrate how your knowledge/area of expertise has helped your client or an organisation you have worked with. If you don't feel comfortable speaking about your client, or if there are legal implications, you can avoid using the client's name or approach them directly to get their permission to be mentioned.

Example: Building thought leadership through LinkedIn – A case study of Company X.

Problem and solution

These blog posts allow you to pose a problem that you think is faced by your target audiences and to solve that problem using your expertise. This type of blog post is a great way to build your credibility as an expert, as you can write about an issue facing your industry and give opinions and solutions.

Example: Many people don't know the logistics of starting a business overseas. Here are some tips on how to open a business bank account in different countries.

Stories

Stories are more personal blog posts and use your personal experiences to convey a point. This is where your creativity can really shine through as it is completely up to you what story you choose to share.

Example: What I learnt about leadership from my mentor.

Curating news

By curating newsworthy content and providing your opinion on it you can build your reputation as an expert. You can also drive traffic to your blog by including keywords that are trending, such as breaking news or industry news people will be searching for.

A blog post curating news will usually give a summary of the news story from the blogger's point of view, followed by commentary and advice.

Example: How SME businesses are likely to be affected by a particular legislation change made by the government.

Content planning

Your blog will not help you achieve your goal of being a recognised thought leader if you post once or twice and forget about it, or put it on the never-ending "to do" list.

There is nothing worse than looking at a blog and the last post was January 2012. (Is that you?!)

Set a posting schedule

Just like a magazine or newspaper, your blog should have a publishing deadline. My blog, PublicRelationsSydney, is updated every Tuesday no matter what is happening in the day. We have never missed an update (although we do have a Christmas break).

If you have a set schedule, it takes the argument "I'm too busy, I'll do it tomorrow (which never comes)" out of the equation. Aim to post at least once per week.

Editorial calendar

Plan ahead and map out a content publishing schedule for 6-12 months in an editorial calendar. An editorial calendar should include the blog post ideas/themes/topics and date. You may find it useful to use an Excel spreadsheet or Google calendar.

It also provides you with an opportunity to identify key business events (i.e. conferences, launches) and post about the events in the lead up or to source available resources such as eBooks or infographics to share.

An editorial calendar is a great way to avoid repeating the same topic. Planning your activities and updates will enable you to share fresh content and ideas with your audience.

It also means you can plan and promote your blog posts ahead of time. For example, you could publish a five-part series on leadership trends for 2015.

It's so much easier to sit down and write when you know what you're writing about.

Set time aside to blog

You may want to block out time in your diary, say every Friday morning, as your time to blog.

Writing tips

Writing for online is very different to writing for print materials. People tend to scan information online and browse sites quickly before making a decision to click through to another page or site.

This means you need to adapt your writing style to suit online reading. It makes it easier for people to quickly understand the essence of your content and captures their attention.

Here are some tips to help you write great online content:

Length

As most people scan read online, posts should be a readable length, such as between 300-600 words. Shorter posts are easier to produce over the long term. Also, it takes much less time to write 600 words, compared to 1,500 words - so you won't procrastinate as much about it!

Keep paragraphs short

Short paragraphs make it easy for people to scan your content, plus they are easier to read on a monitor compared with large blocks of text. Keep your writing concise and avoid repetition and over explanation.

Use subheadings

Subheadings are useful signposts to guide readers through your content and enable easier scanning. Make sure the font is reader friendly, for instance Verdana, and avoid writing in all capitals. Bold all headings and subheadings to make them stand out.

Use dot points where necessary

Dot points allow you to draw attention to the important facts without having to go into large amounts of detail.

Know your audience

Understand your audience and write content that will appeal to them. Don't use jargon, overly descriptive words or too much colloquial language.

Check your spelling and grammar

Check and re-check your content to make sure it is correct. If you are unsure whether there should be a comma, a colon or a semi colon, it is a good idea to consult a grammar guide. Good grammar and spelling ensures professionalism and increases credibility.

Hyperlinks

Hyperlinks are a great way to link to other online content, such as your website, blog, social media channels or maybe an interesting news article. They are also a useful way of providing additional information without having to go into depth on your post.

Content ideas

As you are building your profile as an expert in a specific area, the content needs to be about that topic area. Make sure you are reading about your industry and willing to share your ideas and thoughts.

Create a document where you keep a running list with questions you get from clients, advice you've given clients, customer service questions and questions you've been asked on social media or at a speaking function.

Scan Twitter, Facebook, forums and competitors' posts to see what prospects are asking about. What are people struggling with? What are their triggers?

What goes on behind the scenes? Think about your internal systems or the how's and why's that would be interesting to your readers. For example, I have written about virtually everything we do in our day from how we pitch to journalists, how we put media lists together, to how we put together a social media strategy. You name it, my team and I have written about it.

Quick content tips

- Highlight special products and services.
- Attended an interesting seminar? Put your learning/notes in a blog post.
- Writing a detailed email reply? "Reply to public" with a blog post.
- Answering the same question a second time? Put it in a blog post.
- Learnt something new relating to your industry? Blog about what you learned.
- Read something you don't agree with? Blog about it.
- Note down everything you do in your role. Tell your readers about how you do each task.
- Met someone interesting at an event? Interview them via email and blog about it.

Regular guest bloggers

You can ask other people or bloggers to write a blog post to include on your blog. You can also offer them a guest blogging position where they contribute regular posts to your blog.

Many blogs use regular guest columnists/bloggers as a way of creating content (that the blog doesn't have to produce), attracting readers who follow the guest blogger (especially if they are high profile) and getting quality posts that can be published more frequently. A good example of blogs that use this strategy include Samara Magazine and herBusiness.

If you plan on using this technique, be very clear about the quality of the posts you allow, the topics and frequency.

Brainstorm

Brainstorm story ideas so that you aren't getting to each 'writing day' and trying to figure out what to write about.

If you work in a business, invite people from various divisions to join you to help come up with ideas. Ask them what clients are asking about – knowing what your target audiences are struggling with is key to writing about solutions that solve your readers' issues.

If you're solo, invite clients or friends for a brainstorm or go and sit under a tree, or to your favourite coffee shop.

Set a timer and write down as many ideas as you can in 5 or 10 minutes; don't edit or ponder, just get down as many ideas as you can. Then pick your top 20 and add them to your calendar.

Drive traffic to your blog

One of the most effective ways to drive traffic to your blog is to write often and write well. Sounds simple, but it means that your readers will keep coming back to read your posts. Search engines, such as Google, love fresh content, so you will be ranked higher the more relevant and fresh your content is.

Add share buttons – Great content gets shared more often. Add the "share buttons" at the top of your posts just under the title so your readers can easily and quickly share it.

Use images – Images are important for sharing on social media. Facebook and LinkedIn automatically add an image with the URL which makes the post so much more readable and noticeable.

Share your blog on social media – Make it a LinkedIn status update, tweet a link to a new post (several times), share it on Facebook, or email key people when you blog about a topic of interest to them.

Comment on other blogs – Read other blogs and comment on them so that it links back to your own blog. You can also offer to be a guest blogger on other blogs and websites to increase your exposure. Create an RSS feed of your blog posts to provide an easy way for readers to be updated on new posts.

Tag your posts – Adding metadata to your blog posts (things like the title, the category, tags, etc.) will make a huge difference to how easily that post is found by search engines and, therefore, by the people you want reading your posts.

Offline – Add the blog URL in your email signature and your business card.

Start Blogging

ACTION STEP 9: Write an original post.

ACTION STEP 10: Write a content curated post.

Visit **www.UnknownToExpertBonus.com**
For Your FREE Bonus Action Step Content

Additional **Blog Post Examples** and other valuable content to accelerate your journey from Unknown To Expert available at:

www.UnknownToExpertFaster.com

VALUE: $2000
ONLY $97

Guest blogging

Guest blogging is another cost effective (in other words, free!) promotional strategy you can easily use to build your profile as an expert.

This strategy involves writing and publishing an article on someone else's blog. Depending on the popularity of the blog, your post has the potential to be seen by a huge number of people.

If done right, guest blogging allows you to:

- **Build credibility**: Associating yourself with reputable blogs and having your content appear there will increase your credibility as an expert and help you develop your personal brand.
- **Get your message out to the right and the most relevant audience**: If you do your research and select the right blogs, you will be able to reach a huge audience and, what's more, you will reach the right audience – the people who are most likely to benefit from your experience and expertise.
- **Drive traffic back to your website and/or your blog**: Most guest blogs include either a link back to the expert's blog or even a brief bio about the expert. This means if you do your job well and write the best blog post you possibly can, people will be naturally interested to find out more about you by clicking on the link or Googling you, which is exactly what you want.

How to find blogs

Make a broad list of blogs that fit in with your target market and your target industry. Include formal news style blogs such as LeadingCompany, Mamamia, LifeHacker etc.

The initial list should give you a better idea of the topics people in your target audience are interested in reading and the types of blogs and websites that cover these topics.

The types of blogs that exist have become more and more diversified due to their popularity. There are group blogs that have several contributors;

blogs written by just one person; blogs in the process of becoming online publications who have hired both paid and unpaid staff; debate style blogs which accept submissions from the public; blogs which are online businesses in their own right and many more.

The next step is narrowing down your broad list to the top 10 blogs where you would love to guest blog.

Use the following guidelines to help you make a decision:

- How frequently is the blog updated?
- Has the blog received any media coverage?
- Check how social the blog is. Does it have more than 500 likes on Facebook? Are there comments on blog entries? How active is the Twitter feed (Is there at least one tweet a day?)
- Does this blog provide opportunities for guest blogging or is it written by one person?
- What happens when you google the blog?
- Does this blog have partnerships or receive support from large organisations or associations?

Answering all of these questions will help you assess just how influential a blog is. You don't have to go through this list for each blog. Instead just use it to weed out the blogs you are not sure about.

Approaching bloggers

After you have finalised your guest blogging list, it's time to decide how you are going to approach them.

First decide what you are going to 'offer' – in other words, the content you would like to contribute.

Read the blog and decide on the issue you would like to explore and write about. Make a decision based on the format of the blog and the topics covered. Some blogs make it clear that they do not promote any products, which means you will be better off writing a 'how-to' blog or exploring an issue that will be interesting to the readers.

Once you've figured out your approach (offer), you can begin creating a pitch to send to the blogger.

How to pitch

The pitch should be in the form of an email, which needs to be clear and to the point. Busy people do not read long emails, so clearly outline your idea in the first paragraph.

Take the time to detail the story idea and explain why their readers would be interested in your content.

How to follow up

Bloggers won't always publish a phone number on their site so a follow up phone call is not always possible. If they don't reply to your initial email after a week, send them a follow up email. If they still don't reply you should stop contacting them – they are clearly not interested. Don't annoy them.

What to do once a blogger is interested

When a blogger is interested in receiving a guest blog post ask them for any guidelines they may have about length, format or any deadlines. Make sure what you write is going to be relevant to the audience and not overly promotional, otherwise the blogger will be within their rights to reject your content.

Once you've written your post, make sure that you include:

- Your expert bio.
- A link to your blog or website.
- A high resolution image of yourself.

After sending your blog post to the blogger, make sure to ask them when the post will go live. When it is published promote it on your social networks, in your enewsletter, on your website and on your blog.

Here is an example of a pitch to a blogger:

Hi,

My name is Jane Smith and I'm a business expert in HR and leadership.

I think LeadingCompany is a great resource for businesses and people in business and I really enjoy reading contributed articles from influential people in business such as the article by John Smith about influencing people at work. Providing a space where people can learn such useful skills is an excellent initiative!

I thought you may be interested in a post about how leadership in Australia is being impacted by the lack of female representation at senior levels. I would love to share what I know about this topic and I was wondering whether you offer any guest blogging opportunities on your blog?

Please let me know if you might be interested in accepting a guest blog post about this topic.

Guest Blogging Pitch

Now take action by writing a guest blogging pitch.
Go to your Action Step to get started.

ACTION STEP

Visit **www.UnknownToExpertBonus.com**
For Your FREE Bonus Action Step Content

ACCELERATE YOUR OUTCOME

Additional **Lists of Bloggers Plus a Template for Creating Your Own Blogger Lists** and other valuable content to accelerate your journey from Unknown To Expert available at:
www.UnknownToExpertFaster.com

Networking

In addition to building solid relationships with the media and bloggers, it is also a great idea to begin building and maintaining relationships with your target audiences through pre-established channels, such as associations and networks.

Where you should network will depend on your audience. For example, if your target market is small business, then participate in groups for small business owners such as your local chamber of commerce and/or a small business association. If you want to be known as an expert in women's skin health, start networking at women's groups.

How to become a successful networker

The key to good networking is to go alone. Don't take someone with you for support as you will inevitably use the event as a catch up. If you invite a colleague or friend to attend with you, split up during any networking period and catch up after the event.

Networking is not about selling. In fact it's not about talking. It's about listening. A savvy networker knows that networking and building relationships is about taking the time to find out about others, and from there working out if there is any synergy.

The types of questions you can ask include (very simply): Where do you work? What is your role? How is business? Have you been to this group before?

Good networkers also always follow up those they meet. It's not about getting as many business cards as possible, but connecting with people. Try setting a goal for each event to have two great conversations and to contact them and arrange a coffee meeting to chat in more detail.

12

ACTION STEP

Your Network
Target Industries & Associations

It's time to start your networking planning so you can use your elevator statement and really build your relationships with people that will assist in your thought leadership process. Jump over to the Action Step and list your target industries and associations.

Visit **www.UnknownToExpertBonus.com**
For Your FREE Bonus Action Step Content

Stepping on stage

Being an expert and thought leader means you are a valued speaker for events. Take advantage of this to raise your public profile and promote yourself through finding speaking opportunities for yourself. This tactic will significantly advance your objective of moving from unknown to expert.

Being a guest speaker will give you extra credibility, expose you to your target audiences and certainly increase your profile with people who can assist in building your role as a thought leader.

If you are memorable, informative, entertaining and relevant enough to the audience, they will want to connect with you even after your presentation is over.

Your presentation should be informative and interesting and be adapted to suit your audience. For example, avoid using technical language when your audience has no knowledge of your topic. As for training, if you're not a confident public speaker, get some coaching beforehand to ensure you make the most of each opportunity.

Public speaking can lead to a range of new opportunities for you and generate an increase in consulting hours or speaking opportunities. It will help you to:

Position yourself as an expert

Speaking to an audience gives you automatic credibility on your subject matter. By honing your presentation skills and presenting at multiple events related to your field, you will become well known in your industry and soon people will be contacting you to speak at their events.

Reach your target audiences

Being a speaker at niche events, such as industry conferences or associations, allows you to access a specific audience. This means you could be speaking directly to your target market, who will be interested in booking you for future consulting, speaking or commentary opportunities.

Promote yourself

You should also consider opportunities to further promote yourself at the event, such as supplying your bio for the event website, including your marketing material or book in any gift bags on the day and also giving away plenty of business cards.

Identify networking opportunities

Events are a great opportunity to network with other speakers and attendees. Often members of the audience will be eager to talk to you after your presentation. This is a great time to get their details and determine if they would be interested in working with you in the future.

Different types of speaking opportunities

Presentations

The most obvious and common form of speaking opportunity is a presentation you do on your own for a specified time period. Depending on the event you are speaking at, the time allocated to your presentation can vary from 15 minutes to a couple of hours.

This is something to be mindful of if you are not an experienced speaker. Make sure you find out how long presentations are when you are looking for potential opportunities.

On the other hand, the longer your presentation, the more time you have to make an impact on your audience and to establish an emotional connection.

Panel discussions

Panel discussions take some of the pressure off by placing you alongside other speakers to discuss a specific issue, or several issues. If you are new to presenting, panels are a great place to practice and get used to being in front of large groups of people.

These sessions are usually hosted by a MC who will ask panel members questions throughout the event.

The more conversational format of this style of speaking opportunity can make it easier to bring your personality into the discussion.

If you are looking for, or willing to be part of, a panel discussion you should make sure that you are prepared to answer all questions the mediator may throw at you. Most of the time there will be several topics being discussed and, while they are all going to be based around the same theme, the chances are not every question will be directly relevant to your area of expertise.

Breakfasts

Breakfast speaking events are similar to regular presentation opportunities, however they tend to be shorter and give less opportunity for post event networking, as people usually have to leave for work straight after the presentations. Presentations at these types of events are not likely to last more than 30 minutes. They are also not great if you're not a morning person (like me!).

Luncheons

Lunch time events are organised to include a meal either before or after the presentation. Depending on the event, you may be able to network with the attendees during lunch or have time for extended networking afterwards. These types of events are usually around 30 minutes, and you need to be prepared to speak to an audience of people more interested in their food than you!

Workshops

Speaking opportunities can also be in the form of a workshop where you are involved in the capacity of a mentor or teacher. They involve preparation and require you to actively interact with your attendees over an extended time.

Paid versus unpaid

We would all love to get paid for speaking all of the time, but in my experience that just isn't realistic. When you are starting to build your profile as a thought leader, use speaking opportunities as a way to get in front of your target audiences and develop your reputation. The gain isn't financial at the time, but will certainly lead to new business and new opportunities down the track.

Speaker's profile

If you want to speak, you need a speaker's profile. This document demonstrates your expertise and highlights your speaking experience.

It outlines your bio, the topics you can speak about and any previous public speaking experience you have.

Every time you pitch to speak at an event you should attach the speaker's profile to the email.

Here is an example of my speaker's profile (although I do tailor it depending on the event).

SPEAKER'S PROFILE

Catriona Pollard

Director, CP Communications

Catriona is passionate about social media, public relations, business and bringing them all together to create real, financial success for entrepreneurs and organisations.

Catriona is renowned for being an inspiring presenter that shares practical skills and expertise so attendees can immediately implement what they've learnt to see real results.

Catriona Pollard is the founder and director of CP Communications one of Sydney's most respected and innovative boutique PR and social media agencies.

An expert in developing public relations and social media strategies that engage consumers as well as businesses, she has developed and implemented strategies for hundreds of organisations including Hilton Australasia, Macquarie University, The Jumbana Group, Lego, City of Sydney as well as many up and coming companies.

As an early adopter of social media in the Australian PR industry she is an advocate of Twitter, Facebook, LinkedIn and blogs. Catriona writes the popular blog Public Relations Sydney that led to her being labelled as a leading public relations blogger. Public Relations Sydney is also listed as the top two business blog in Australia. Catriona is also listed as one of the top 100 PR people worldwide to follow on Twitter.

Catriona regularly provides comments to the media about public relations and social media and teaches a course she designed called PR and Media releases that get results at the Australian Writers' Centre. She also authors articles on PR and social media which are extensively published online and in print.

Catriona has written ebooks 'How to use PR to get Amazing results' and 'Your Guide to Social Media Success' and published 'Unknown to Expert: How to Use Clever PR and Social Media to Become a Thought leader.'

Speaking Topics

- **Powerful PR for visible businesses**

Reputation is the new currency and you need a bucket load of it for your business to be visible to your target audiences.

With a good reputation you can build your customers' trust in your business, leading to more sales and business opportunities.

In this presentation Catriona will discuss why it's vital for business leaders to understand public relations and how it can help their business to achieve results.

This presentation is a must for every business leader and manager striving to lead an organisation in today's challenging and volatile market.

From this presentation attendees will learn:

- ✓ What is PR and it can help you to achieve your business goals.
- ✓ Why online communication like blogging and social media is the new marketing frontier.
- ✓ Why building a profile and reputation matters and why doing good work is no longer enough to win new clients.
- ✓ Examples of how successful organisations have used PR to get results.

- **Building a personal brand with PR**

Being known as an expert in your industry can be incredibly powerful for your reputation as well as the reputation of your business. This presentation will share the secret behind building a strong personal brand that will highlight you as a go-to expert and a leader in your field.

We all have stories to tell. Personal stories, professional stories, stories that let people know who we are, what we stand for, what we do. By using tried and tested PR tactics, Catriona will discuss the things every business leader can do to building a credible personal brand that will get noticed and respected.

From this presentation attendees will learn:

- ✓ How to develop your personal brand.
- ✓ What PR tactics you can use to become known as an expert in your field.
- ✓ How to successfully pitch yourself to the media to share your stories and raise awareness of your brand.
- ✓ What online tools, like blogging and social media, you can use to increase your visibility.
- ✓ Lots of helpful tips and tricks of the trade to help you grow your brand.

- **Understanding the power of social media**

Social media is a powerful communication tool, which businesses can use to communicate with their target audiences, gain valuable customer feedback and build their brand awareness. Businesses need to understand how they can leverage the power of social media to achieve their business goals.

From this presentation attendees will learn:

- ✓ What are the best social media tools for your business and how to use them?
- ✓ How to create and post quality content.
- ✓ How to create engagement on social media.

Previous speaking experience

Catriona regularly speaks on PR and social media.

Here are few examples:

ProBlogger – DIY PR to grow your blog and your brand

Digital Marketing Forum

Women on Boards – You are your best PR

CEO Institute – LinkedIn Seminar

Women In Focus – Blogging Bootcamp

Country Women's Association – Publicity seminar

City of Sydney – Social media for your career

Macquarie University – Social media and personal branding workshop

Commonwealth Bank – Women in Focus conference – PR and social media

Little Black Dress Group – PR workshop

The CEO Institute – PR workshop and LinkedIn workshop

Macquarie University Women and Leadership conference – Putting Me into social media

Australian Writers' Centre – Teaches a regular one-day course on PR and social media

Testimonials from previous speaking engagements

"Love listening to passionate people talk about what they love, brilliant workshop" – **Sarah Riegelhuth**

"Catriona brought alive some real communication possibilities, lighting up the faces in the room as they saw beyond the unknown and alienating technical jargon of social media. This opened up a room of challenges – but also an ocean of possibilities and opportunities. The room was engrossed. Through offering practical tips and simple steps Catriona left people excited and inspired, with new worlds beckoning and all asking for more." - **Anitra Morgana, Executive Officer, Leichhardt & Annandale Business Chamber**

"Catriona was a fantastic presenter with lots of great applied examples of lessons." - **Nicole Miller**

"Catriona was warm, friendly and receptive to all comments/questions. It's very encouraging to hear success stories (as well as what's unsuccessful) from someone so experienced, and her confidence is definitely contagious." - **Annie Vaughan**

"Excellent - Catriona has an inclusive, friendly style that, at the same time, is commercially very savvy." - **Natasha Brooks**

"Loved your workshop at the Women In Leadership Conference. I now appreciate the importance of social media." – **Karen Mizzi**

Media coverage

Catriona regularly provides expert comments to the media on PR and social media. She has been featured hundreds of publications. Here are a few examples:

- Management Today: How to position yourself as a thought leader

- Women's Agenda: Tips for Women in Leadership that I wish someone had told me

- B&T: Is storytelling the emperor's new clothes?

- Business Director Magazine: Generation Social

- Professional Marketing: Who has the cleverest marketing campaign

- Sydney Morning Herald: Five ways to switch off

- Management Today: What you need to know about Google+

- SmartCompany: Small businesses have an edge as larger rivals piece together social media puzzle

- CEO Magazine: Making the most of LinkedIn

- The Australian.com.au: Social media train's at the station

- LeadingCompany – regular contributor: Social media no room for naysayers

About CP Communications

CP Communications, a PR and social media agency which provides specialist media, traditional and online PR strategies that achieve positive media coverage, increased brand awareness and improved sales results.

What sets CP Communications apart is their approach. They don't pump out press releases all day. They believe that good PR is more clever than that. Good PR is about asking the right questions, understanding the landscape of the media and market, and having an antenna poised to pick up on any opportunities to benefit our client's business.

Clients describe them as "absolute professionals who are always on the lookout for new ideas and points of difference". Journalists say, "if only there were more PR companies like CP Communications!"

cpcommunications
public relations | social media

Catriona Pollard Communications Pty Ltd

Suite 404, 10-12 Clarke Street, Crows Nest NSW 2065

P: (02) 9460 9200

E: cp@cpcommunications.com.au

W: www.cpcommunications.com.au

S: www.socialmediasydney.net.au

Blog: www.PublicRelationsSydney.com.au

T: @catrionapollard and @CPCPR

F: www.facebook.com/cpcommunications

L: www.linkedin.com/in/catrionapollard

Y: http://www.youtube.com/publicrelationstips

P: http://pinterest.com/cpcpr/

G: http://bit.ly/CPCGoogle

Your Speaker Profile

If you want to start speaking you absolutely need to have a professional speaker's profile. So now take the time to develop your own profile. Remember, without action it's very hard to achieve results – so take action.

Visit **www.UnknownToExpertBonus.com**
For Your FREE Bonus Action Step Content

How to find speaking opportunities

Once you have your speaker's profile, you need to do some research about where you want to speak. Have a think about where your target audiences are and what they are interested in.

Begin by making a list of the different associations, chambers, clubs and organisations that focus on your subject matter and area of expertise. For example, if you were an expert in retailing you could contact the National Retail Association and the Australian Retailers Association.

There are also conferences, large and small, held all over the country throughout the year on every subject. You need to become familiar with these. Do some online research around the keywords relating to your topics of expertise. Search for stand-alone conferences and events that are scheduled in 3-6 months from when you would like to present (as they book speakers well in advance).

Industry bodies will also usually hold annual conferences. For example AIMIA, the Digital Industry Association for Australia, holds a Digital Summit around the same time every year.

You can also become a member of associations relevant to your area of expertise, as many of these associations give preference to members as opposed to speakers from the general public.

Do you know someone who is an expert in an area similar to yours? Take look at their website and they will probably list their previous speaking engagements.

Another place to look at is networking groups - the larger ones often invite guest speakers as a reason for people to get together to do networking.

Here are some tips on where to look for speaking opportunities:

Large events and conferences

September is usually when event organisers start planning the event program for the coming year. Larger speaking events take anywhere from half a year to a year to organise so you should get in early. Send your profile to the event organisers even before all the information (such as cut-off dates and the event program) is available. Usually if you hold off until all the details have been put up, it's too late.

Associations and chambers

Associations and chambers tend to need speakers on an ongoing basis. The event organisers are less concerned with filling a program within their deadlines and more concerned with delivering what their members want. Before pitching for these types of speaking opportunities study their websites to find out who has spoken previously and what topics have been covered.

Networking groups

Like associations and chambers, networking groups need speakers on an ongoing basis. They are less rigid about their guest speakers and tend to choose interesting stories and angles. Of course they still have to fit in with the group's target audience and subject matter.

How to pitch to speaking opportunities

When you have compiled a list of potential speaking spots, it's time to find out more information. There is no point spending time pitching to all of these places only to find out that they are not the right fit for you, regardless of how appropriate they might appear to begin with.

Call and ask to speak to the event organiser of the potential speaking opportunity. When you get them on the phone explain that you would like to put yourself forward as a potential speaker for their upcoming event but would like to find out more information first.

The following are some questions to help you decide if an opportunity is right for you:

- Are there speaking opportunities available?
- What kind of speakers are you looking for? Anyone in a particular industry with particular expertise?
- How many people are you expecting to attend?

- What industries are the attendees mostly from?
- What are the positions of the attendees who come along?
- How long is the presentation?
- Is there time for networking before or after the event?

All of these questions should help you decide if this is the right speaking opportunity for you, and if you are the right speaker for the opportunity.

You don't have to ask every single one of these questions, especially if the answers can be found online, however they are good guidelines to keep in mind.

Creating your speaker pitch

As mentioned earlier, each speaker pitch you send out should be customised to the speaking opportunity.

Make sure you get the name of the event organiser and spell it correctly when sending your pitch. It's a small detail but it can make a big difference to the receiver.

Write an introduction offering yourself as a speaker and summarising your expertise which will be relevant for the audience. It's a good idea to list three key issues you can cover.

Then provide an abstract of the topic you would like to speak about at the event. Make sure you edit the abstract to make it fit in with the audience and their needs. For example, if the audience is from the education sector and you are talking about marketing an education provider to students, don't refer to them as customers. Change the term to 'potential students' or 'stakeholders'.

Finish your pitch by explaining that the speaker's profile is attached and ask the organisers to let you know if they would be interested in having you speak at the event.

Here is an example of an email pitch which aims at gaining a speaking engagement.

Hi #,

It was great to speak to you on the phone about XX event. As discussed here is some more information.

As director of CP Communications, a PR and social media agency, I am an expert in public relations and social media with 18 years experience in developing and managing PR and social media strategies across a range of industries, particularly B2B.

I am renowned for being an inspiring presenter who shares practical skills and expertise so attendees can immediately implement what they've learnt to see real results.

I am frequently asked to speak at a range of conferences and events on PR, social media and business strategies.

Here is my suggested speaking topic:

Connect, Share & Build - PR & social media for your business

Both PR and social media are tools you can use to tell your company's stories. Every organisation has stories to tell, and amazing stories deserve a good audience.

In this session, public relations and social media expert, Catriona Pollard, will cover how to identify your stories and tools to share them with large numbers of people who can influence the perception of your brand and organisation.

She will discuss how to leverage the opportunities in both social media and public relations to effectively build your business' profile and reputation.

Learn how to develop story ideas that you can pitch to the media and how to implement tactics including media angles and article writing. Learn a step-by-step guide to social media and discover how you can use it to increase the profile, credibility and reputation for your business – and yourself.

I have attached my speaking profile, testimonials and additional speaking topics.

I can speak on a range of issues related to public relations and social media, please let me know if you are interested in any of my speaking topics.

Creating Your Speaker Pitch

14

ACTION STEP

Create your speaker pitch.
Open your Action Step and start now.

Visit **www.UnknownToExpertBonus.com**
For Your FREE Bonus Action Step Content

ACCELERATE YOUR OUTCOME

Additional **Checklist for Speaking Opportunities** and other valuable content to accelerate your journey from Unknown To Expert available at:

www.UnknownToExpertFaster.com

Following up

Follow up by phone two weeks after you have sent your pitch. If the event organiser is not interested ask for their feedback about why you weren't successful.

If you were successful, ask them for the next steps. Sometimes event organisers will need you to sign a speaker agreement. Other times you may need to sign a confidentiality agreement (if you are speaking to a CEO audience for example).

After you have formally accepted your speaking spot you may be provided with a complete list of attendees, which should help you do some targeted networking at the event as well as provide you with the opportunity to connect with them on LinkedIn.

Speaking opportunity checklist

To keep track of all of the details of your speaking opportunities, it's a good idea to create a speaking opportunity checklist for each event. This should include the date, time, topic, location, contact details and more.

Tips for public speaking

The main purpose of public speaking is to communicate your message to your target audience in an engaging way to encourage them to remember it. Public speaking can help to build your profile as an expert in your industry and increase your target audience's brand awareness.

Here are some tips to help you improve your public speaking skills:

- Regardless of what the event is, make sure you arrive at least 15 minutes early to set up.
- Always have a backup plan for your presentation. Things can go wrong and you should be prepared for them to go wrong.
- Think about how to respond to negative comments or difficult questions.
- Have your business cards with you.
- Have water handy.

Prepare and practice

Before a public speaking opportunity it is essential to do some research into the topic you want to discuss and the main points you will communicate. The more knowledge you have about your topic the more confident you will be.

You can then thoroughly prepare your speech and practice, practice, practice. When you know what you are talking about there will be less room for error.

Know the audience and the venue

Before your presentation find out who the audience will be and how much knowledge they will have on your topic so you can pitch it at the right level. It is essential that you tailor the presentation to the bulk of the audience and understand what makes them tick and what drives them.

Familiarising yourself with the audience and venue is a great way to decrease any nervous tension. Get to the venue early, and speak to some audience members. Also check that your audio-visual and PowerPoint/

Prezi presentation is working effectively.

Relax and deliver

When speaking to an audience it's important to relax and be yourself. If you feel nervous, use relaxation techniques such as controlled breathing to calm your nerves, make sure you are prepared, practice plenty of times and be strong in your delivery.

Use efficient body language

Remember, 93 percent of communication is non-verbal. The audience will not just be looking at your face; they will be looking at your body as well. Be confident in what you say; stand up straight, look at the audience, and smile from time to time. Put your hands by your side, not in your pockets and not behind your back.

Don't forget to dress properly and be comfortable as well. Getting your point across means showing the audience you are confident. Remember, presentation is not what is said but *how* it's said.

Don't read, deliver

Nothing is worse than listening to a speech where the presenter is reading the entire time. If you want to get the attention of your audience you must keep the presentation interesting. Add some humour, talk to the audience, and use some visual aids.

The purpose of the speech is to be relatable; the audience has to identify with you in some way. If you are reading the whole time, you are not identifying with the audience and your presentation will become meaningless.

Become a regular public speaker

The more you practice public speaking, the more successful you will be. With practice you can also learn how to control your nerves and become more confident.

Start by speaking at small events and then build up to bigger conferences.

Accept any opportunity possible to practice your public speaking and believe in what you are saying. The more practice you do, the better your public speaking will become and you will be more successful in delivering your message.

Developing as a public speaker

Practice, of course, makes perfect but you can also invest in some public speaking training, such as:

- **Toastmasters** – A world-renowned method of becoming a better speaker. The true value of Toastmasters lies in its practicality. The club gives you the opportunity to develop speaking skills through pure practice and constructive feedback from other members of the club.
- **Coaching** – If you have the budget you can hire a speaking coach who can help you with everything from structuring your presentation, to using body language and your voice effectively.
- **Acting classes** – Even if you have no intention of ever acting, acting classes are also a great way of gaining confidence on stage and practicing your presentation skills. Quite often acting classes involve impromptu exercises, which can help you not be caught off guard if you forget what to say.

Use the Media to
Shine the Light

At Star 4 if you've done the work, this is where you'll see your role as an expert take shape. Start to use the media to share your expertise, your stories and reach the people that will influence your success.

The media love experts and thought leaders. They need them for their articles and programs, as they provide the credibility, opinions and commentary.

Journalists are always looking for experts in a particular field to provide professional comments or quotes for their story. But you need to be visible, and you need to be proactive.

PR is so successful because it provides a journalist with an objective view about your company. PR is also an effective method of communicating with your customers to build a relationship with them.

The first step is to use PR strategies to build up your status as an expert and understand how to offer your professional knowledge to a journalist.

In this section I'll be covering the many techniques involved in a PR strategy which you can use to move from unknown to recognised expert.

Getting the media interested

Have you ever wondered why a story was in the news? Or how the media decides what stories are worth covering?

The media looks for stories that have news value. For a story to be considered newsworthy it is likely to have one of the following five factors:

1. **Timing:** A story must be new and current. Generally, a story is newsworthy if it happened today, but not if it happened last month.

2. **Prominence:** Prominent people, celebrities and well-known companies are newsworthy.

3. **Human interest:** These stories appeal to human emotion and aim to evoke an emotional response, such as sadness or amusement.

4. **Significance:** This relates to how many people the story affects. A story that affects a lot of people is more newsworthy than a story that only affects a small group of people.

5. **Proximity:** Where the story occurred. Journalists are more interested in local stories than stories about other countries, states or regions.

Another important consideration is the news agenda. The competition between stories for news coverage will have an effect on whether a story will run.

For instance, if a major news story breaks such as a local natural disaster, then most of the news stories for that day will be about the natural disaster. This means your newsworthy story may be bumped for an even better story. On a slow news day, you may have a better chance of getting coverage because there is less competition.

Identifying story angles

A story angle is a unique story idea related to your business which you can pitch into a journalist. A great angle will leverage one or many of the five factors, discussed previously, which make a story newsworthy.

Journalists get hundreds of story angles across their desk each day. How do you know what makes a good story angle and how do you make yours stand out over the others?

The experts can look at an organisation and find aspects that will make great stories the media will love. As an expert, you need to learn how to look at your expertise and background from an outsider's point of view and decide which areas people may want to know about.

There is no guarantee that when you send a story idea to a journalist they are going to run with it. However, you have a much better chance if you go the extra mile - research every show or publication before you send your pitch, and give it a targeted, relevant, timely story angle.

Key tips to developing story angles

Here are some tips that will help you develop those story ideas:

Read the daily paper

This sounds really obvious, but get into the habit of reading newspapers (online or printed). Scan the headlines of each section and ask yourself, "What is in the news today that ties in with what I want to promote?"

Read the publications you want your story in

Reading through the publications you want to be featured in will give you a good idea about what stories they are looking for and what sections they have. Once you have figured out their agenda, you can either pitch in stories or write articles for the specific sections.

Listen to questions your clients and customers ask you

Are you suddenly hearing lots of people asking the same question? If you are on Twitter, are you noticing a trending topic that relates to your area of expertise? Can you make a comment about this trending topic which would be interesting to targeted journalists or bloggers?

Read industry publications to spot industry trends

What is the buzz in your industry (trade) publications? Are there new developments in your field that you can provide comment on or develop into a story idea? Use your access to this information and expertise in your industry to shape a story. This is a great way of building your profile within your industry and amongst your peers.

Media angle ideas

Use surveys to craft story ideas: The media views quantitative data as newsworthy and accurate. Launch a survey or piggyback on survey results that relate to your industry to create a strong story. If you are using your own survey, ensure it has enough respondents to make it useable.

Leap on breaking news relevant to your industry as a chance to put yourself in the news.

Human interest: Personal story as the inspiration behind a business start-up, rags to riches. Highlight that you're doing something most people are afraid to attempt, such as starting a business during a recession.

Employees: new appointment staff, board director.

Milestones: 10th year in business.

Business Development: new product/services, new contract win, new store opening.

Give evergreen stories topical new hooks: Have you noticed that New Year's resolution articles fill newspapers and magazines every January and tax tips abound in March? Editors always have a need for evergreen stories, but need fresh twists and hooks that are relevant to their audiences. A "top ten" list of tips is always welcome.

Create your own special day: Create a story angle by tying in with regular holidays or with a little-known but highly relevant holiday. You can even make up your own special day or week and get publicity for it.

Provide actual users of your service or product for the media to interview. Their testimonials will boost your credibility.

Provide a journalist with an expert to interview who has used and can vouch for your product. If you sell skin cream, for example, ask a dermatologist who likes your product to be available for an interview.

Embrace anything that makes you unique.

Look for sections in the newspaper that highlight interesting businesses, often under headlines like "What's That Business." Normally a simple phone call with a pitch will secure a feature on your business.

Achievements – What have you achieved? Have you won an award? Let journalists know. They won't be interested in mundane activities such as employee of the month, but they will care if it is interesting and a big deal.

Other examples

- Top 10 tips to..
- Staff retention and engagement initiatives
- Speaker at public or industry event
- Official launch of a new business
- New business to meet special market niche
- Market research led to a new business idea
- New product/service available/soon to be launched
- New store opening or interstate expansion
- Won an industry/service award
- Statistics to show business growth
- Longest serving employee reached XXth year
- Sponsoring employees for further education
- Unique employee trainee program
- Work/life balance initiatives
- Creation of long-term relationship with local or well-known charity
- Leading industry innovation by implementing XXX
- Introduction of environmentally-friendly methodology/technology

Media angle examples for a Mobile Marketing Company

At my Agency we regularly brainstorm story ideas for a client where the whole team will come up with ideas for a specific client or topic. Here is the result of one we did for a mobile marketing company. These were then used for articles, media pitches, presentation topics and media releases.

- Incorporating m-commerce into your business plans
- Understanding the ROI of mobile
- Customer experience on android – why it is behind iOS
- How mobile can make loyalty more cost effective
- Pros & cons of apps for businesses
- The business case for going mobile
- Cross-platform optimisation as a revenue driver for business – generating apps across all platforms (iPhones, iPads, Android, windows, Firefox, safari etc.) – opportunity to use a case study if they have done this for a client.
- Optimisation is only half the battle – Businesses must be testing their apps
- Why CEOs should understand mobile marketing to manage it correctly in the business
- How consumers are purchasing products now and how to adjust marketing to their needs (m-commerce)
- Tapping into niches through mobile marketing (more effective niche marketing)
- Commentary on the retail industry – why mobile marketing is a great opportunity for smaller Australian retailers who need to innovate to survive, now is the time for mobile
- Why mobiles are becoming the biggest marketing medium since TV
- How to use mobile apps and mobile websites for internal processes and efficiency – not just a marketing tool
- Forget your traditional website, just go mobile
- How to decide on an app to market your business
- How mobile can become a core marketing solution – not just an add on

- Invigorate your marketing with mobile
- Functionality vs. design – where to draw the line?
- 4G: what it means for your mobile marketing
- Is mobile saving retail?
- Internal vs. external – why not all apps have to be created for customers
- New interactive ways to differentiate your marketing efforts – text to screen, SMS to email (interactive messaging)
- What does creating an app involve? (How to make it, who to make it, how to get on the iPhone App Store, design for android vs. iPhone etc.)
- What's your business's 5 year goal – how can mobile marketing help you achieve it?
- Transferring offline loyalty programs to online – the process and what it involves
- Why CEOs should understand mobile
- Budget and mobile marketing – how much money you need
- When to go mobile – how do you know you should have a mobile site?
- Mobile website v apps – how are they different and which one should you use and when?
- Why mobile works – the reason behind why it's effective
- Top 5 productivity apps – why they work

Media Angle Brainstorm

Now use whatever brainstorming method works for you: Sitting under a tree, turning on some music, going to a noisy cafe, chatting with colleagues/friends and open your Action Step and start.

Visit **www.UnknownToExpertBonus.com**
For Your FREE Bonus Action Step Content

Dealing with the media

Public relations is a marathon, not a sprint, and the best way to ensure you move from unknown to recognised expert is to build genuine relationships with the media.

Journalists work in a fast-paced, high-pressure environment. They constantly receive media releases, phone calls and emails about the latest and greatest products or business ideas.

So to make sure you are noticed and start building solid relationships with journalists, here are a few tips for you to follow:

Know the publication

If you want to pitch a story idea to a publication, you should be consistently reading it. This will help you to know the style of the publication, the different journalists and what they write about. It's no use pitching a story about health for women to a journalist who writes about accounting.

Also make sure your pitch fits the media's target market. No matter how good you think the new line of lawn mowers you are selling is, it's probably not something Woman's Day magazine is ever going to run with. If you pitch something completely out of place, the journalist is more likely to ignore you the next time you send them something.

Pick your time wisely

A bit of research and common sense can tell you when a media outlet's deadline is. Daily papers will obviously have a deadline each day so getting your information to a journalist earlier in the day may be an advantage for you as you'll be contacting them when the stress is a bit less. Monthly publications, such as some magazines, have long lead times and can be looking for articles months in advance. So there is no point contacting a magazine at the end of the month trying to get into the next month's issue.

Send it to one person per publication only

Sending a media release to a range of journalists is a good way to get coverage, but don't send it to several journalists at the same publication at the same time. News rooms are a small place and they will find out.

Make them want to know more

Whether you are sending them a media release or pitching an article over the phone, make sure to present the most interesting information first. The information will have to be tailored for different types of media (e.g. community newspapers are generally only interested in something to do with their immediate area). Media releases won't be read all the way through if the journalist isn't interested from the beginning.

Get the journalist's name right

One of the biggest mistakes you can make is sending an email to Amanda Smith starting with 'Hi Alison.' If you can't even get their name right, what else did you get wrong? Even spelling a name incorrectly is a big no-no, it's a basic courtesy to spell someone's name correctly. Check the publication, or ring them to double-check if you're not sure.

Personalise your pitch

Whether emailing or calling, do a bit of research first and find out which journalist you may wish to speak to. Simply using someone's name can get their attention, make them feel like you have put in a bit of effort and assure them they aren't just calling every media outlet in the country.

Stick to the deadline

If a journalist asks you for a high-res colour image by Friday 3pm, you send them a high-res colour image by Friday 3pm. Not delivering on something you promised a journalist is a sure-fire way to get them to put you on a 'do not accept calls from' list. A journalist is relying on you to help them present a story, completed before deadline. You can't leave them with a space to fill at the last minute.

Don't be afraid of journalists

Journalists have good days and bad days and there are ones who will be nicer than others. But don't be intimidated by them if they are less than sugar and spice, they will respect you more for not sounding nervous. If you contact them at a bad time apologise once and move on. Apologising more than that can become annoying. If you have all your information at hand, know what you are talking about and are polite at all times, you should be received well.

Tactic 1: Media releases

Media releases are often the first thing that comes to mind when discussing public relations. They are a tried and true method and are often very successful.

Journalists also get hundreds of them a day – most of them completely unrelated to their area of interest.

Before you start to write a media release, stop and think about what you want to achieve. Which publication do you want to be covered in? Who is your intended audience? What story do you want to tell? Then decide whether a media release is definitely the right way to go.

When to write a media release

Media releases are appropriate when releasing news about time sensitive issues. A media release helps you communicate your news to a number of key targeted journalists at the same time. This can help you get media coverage in a variety of publications within a certain time frame to ensure you reach your target audience with your news.

Here are some times when you should write a media release:

- **Issues and trends in your industry:** For example, if you have conducted an industry survey and you want to release the findings to your whole industry.
- **Launch of a new product:** You can write a media release detailing the features of your new product, such as a book.
- **Winning an award:** If you win an award, you can share your success and also promote your services with a media release.

When writing a media release you need to keep in mind the publication you will be sending it to. Your overall goal for sending out a media release is to communicate your messages to your target audience. This means you need to target the right journalists and the right publications that your target audiences read.

How to write a media release

The main rule is that all media releases have to be newsworthy. If a media release isn't newsworthy, then it simply won't get picked up. What makes items newsworthy differs greatly from one publication to the next, or even from one section to the next. News is something new, up-to-the minute and of interest to the readers.

Make sure you write your media release in short sentences, short paragraphs and keep the information simple and to the point. Try to keep the media release to one page. A good media release will also have no typographical or grammatical errors.

The media release template

MEDIA RELEASE

Date

- Headline

The headline of a media release should summarise the key points, but be catchy, interesting and strong. It is designed to catch attention and encourage further reading. Ensure you bold it.

- Lead

The lead paragraph is the key part of your media release. It is essential that your lead is punchy and has the story hook. Check that is includes: who, what, when, where, why and how.

- Body

The paragraph under the lead should expand on the lead and be the point where you start telling the story. It is important to prioritise messages from the most important to the least important. Use short sentences and short paragraphs with vigorous, active language. Always write in the third person.

Use quotes to make your writing more interesting but remember all opinions must be attributed to a particular person or the organisation. The media is unable to use newsworthy assertions unless sourced, and journalists will sometimes call to check on the quotes.

- End

The last paragraph is the least important and can include background information about you and your services or summarise the essential elements of the media release.

Always finish the media release with -ends- so the journalist knows it is finished.

- Contact information

Make sure you include the following contact information.

For further media information contact:

Contact name

Email

Phone number

- Boiler plate (About you and your business)

It is important to include a boiler plate at the bottom of your media release. A boiler plate is a one paragraph summary of background information about yourself and your business. This information will give the journalist an overview and isn't necessarily needed in the body of the media release.

Here is an example media release:

MEDIA RELEASE

(date)

The Jumbana Group and Accor team up to build better reconciliation strategies

Accor Hotel and Resorts' recent strategic review of its Indigenous employment program and reconciliation initiatives, by leading Indigenous consulting and communications company, The Jumbana Group, is the latest development in Accor's commitment to reconciliation.

Accor is the world's largest hotel operator and leading hotel employer in Australia. The company has been established in Australia for over

20 years, has a network of over 160 hotels and employs 7,000 people. Since 2001, Accor has employed over 700 Aboriginal and Torres Strait Islanders.

According to Managing Director for The Jumbana Group, Ros Moriarty, Accor is leading the way in a space where Reconciliation Action Plans (RAPs) can be token gestures.

"Accor has been in the RAP space for more than a decade and has undertaken initiatives like nation-wide Indigenous issues workshops for management teams."

"This latest Indigenous Strategic Review focuses on mentoring and other forms of pastoral care in order to provide highly necessary personalised support to Indigenous recruits, with a view to creating the first Indigenous Hotel General Manager in the group," said Ms Moriarty.

Accor developed its Reconciliation Action Plan in 2011 but has been active in supporting Indigenous initiatives for over 10 years. Its RAP comprises of actions and measures by which the company can fulfil its reconciliation commitments based on Relationship, Respect and Opportunities.

Accor's RAP is focused on closing the employment gap between Aboriginal and Torres Strait Islander and non-Indigenous Australians. The company provides training and leadership development by partnering with Indigenous businesses, such as The Jumbana Group, increasing knowledge about Indigenous culture through community involvement and providing opportunities through education and scholarships.

John McDonnell, General Manager HR Asia Pacific at Accor, said the company strives to be a supportive employer, committed to promoting diversity and helping staff to progress and reach their full potential through various training and educational programs.

"We've had a very successful partnership with The Jumbana Group which started in 2012 when they helped us to conduct cultural competency training with Accor's management teams. Our partnership with Jumbana is now centred on moving forward from a focus on recruitment, to better addressing engagement and retention, supporting Accor's position as an industry leader in the reconciliation space," said Mr McDonnell.

Accor's vision for reconciliation covers three key areas: continue to build respect for Indigenous Australians through cultural awareness and activities that build a shared pride in Aboriginal and Torres Strait Islander culture; consolidate existing relationships while building new relationships that support Indigenous employment and engagement; and identify further opportunities to engage and retain Indigenous employees through training and career development.

-ENDS-

For further information or interviews please contact:

Name

CP Communications

Phone: ##

Email: ##

About The Jumbana Group

The Jumbana Group is a leading indigenous art, strategy and communications company which is famously responsible for conceptualising Aboriginal art on Qantas 747 and 737s. The Jumbana Group has been operating for 30 years and comprises of Jumbana Consulting, design studio Balarinji and not-for-profit, The Nangala Project. www.jumbana.com.au

About Accor Hotel and Resorts

Accor, the world's largest hotel operator and leading hotel employer in Europe, currently operates in 90 countries, with more than 4,200 hotels and employs over 145,000 people. The Accor Group offers to its clients and partners nearly 45 years of know-how and expertise. http://accorhotels.com.au/

How to send your media release

Using the media list you will develop a little later on, you will email out the media release in the body of an email. The reason you don't attach the release is because it may get caught by spam and you want the journalist to be able to quickly scan it to see if it's relevant to them. Even one click may mean they don't look at your release.

I don't suggest mass emailing or BCCing media releases. Either use mail merge or send individual emails to the journalists on your list addressing it directly to them (using their first name). Use direct email addresses (no editor@ or info@).

If you want to include an image, embed it in the body of the email (low resolution) and don't attach a high res image.

The subject line of the email is: media release/information with the title of media release and include a brief introduction which contains the media hook.

Here is an example of an email pitching a media release followed by the media release:

Subject: Media Release: Matt Sterne joins Edge as Executive Creative Director

Hi <name>

I thought you might be interested in the below media release announcing the appointment of Matt Stern as the new Executive Creative Director for content agency, Edge.

Matt is Edge's first Executive Creative Director and brings with him big agency experience

Please let me know if I can provide any images of Matt or arrange an interview with Matt or Fergus, Edge's Commercial Director.

Many thanks

(name)

MEDIA RELEASE

<date>

Matt Sterne joins Edge as Executive Creative Director

Content agency Edge, today announced the appointment of Matt Sterne to the position of Executive Creative Director.

With a background in digital, Sterne's key objective will be bringing his creative experience and outside the box thinking to help Edge remain at the forefront of the branded content space.

"There's a perception that only the bigger agencies produce quality work however I took the position with Edge because I could see they were really leading the way in the hot topic of branded content," said Sterne.

"Edge's heritage in editorial was a real draw card as it sets them apart. They are masters of storytelling which shows in the quality of work and the results they produce," added Sterne.

Sterne is Edge's first creative director.

Edge Commercial Director, Fergus Stoddart said, "Bringing Matt on board is a real tipping point for Edge. Over the last several years we have evolved from custom magazines to delivering content campaigns across multiple platforms and Matt's appointment gives us even more creative fire power."

"Matt brings over 13 years of agency experience to this position as well as a strong background in digital marketing. We are delighted to have such a talented and experienced Creative Director join the team," added Mr Stoddart.

Matt joins Edge after more than a decade in digital and more recently, making the crossover to integrated with stints at agencies such as LOWE, HAVAS Worldwide and GPY&R Group.

-ends-

For further information or interviews please contact:

\#

CP Communications

Phone: 02 9460 9200

Email: \#

About Edge

Edge is a strategic content agency creating and producing custom content for brands across any channel or platform, including print, digital, gaming and broadcast. Edge has a strong heritage in quality editorial products and advertising sales, having started in 2003 as a custom magazine publisher.

Edge client's include St George, BMW, Austar, Colliers International, Regional Express and Carnival Australia. The company has offices in Sydney, Melbourne and Perth. www.edgecustom.com.au

Other places to post your media release

After emailing your media release to the media, it's now time to take advantage of social media and online. Here are some great places to upload your media release to increase the amount of views it receives:

Your website or blog

Post your media release as a blog entry or update to your website. As your main online hub, it's a great way to reach your target audience online.

Social media

The next section covers social media in detail, however take note that once you have posted your media release to your website or blog share the link to the post via your social media platforms.

- When tweeting ensure you use hashtags.

- When Facebooking ensure your status update is accompanied by an image – images will always generate more attention than just words.
- When posting to LinkedIn ensure you are only posting from your profile – do not spam groups with your media release.

Tactic 2: The perfect pitch

One of the most successful ways of getting the media interested is coming up with a story angle for their media outlet and pitching them the idea.

You may not realise it, but much of what you see and read in the media are stories which have been provided to the journalist via a PR consultant or person suggesting the idea to the journalist.

Your story idea is more specific than a media release topic. It could be commentary about trends in your industry or your opinion on a specific issue.

You can pitch via email or phone, however before making contact develop a clear outline of your story and ensure it is succinct and compelling.

It should never be a blatant advertisement or advertorial. Simply writing "I'm an expert in xyz, so you should interview me" simply won't cut it! Rather, outline the great story that you have to tell the journalist and why it is relevant to the media by following these steps.

Pitching tips

Tailored pitch

Think about what the readers of the publication (or viewers/listeners of a program) you will be pitching to are interested in. Story angles can include: identifying a problem and giving a solution, suggesting a new approach, describing the lessons learnt from a project and their applications to other areas or even how to do what you do.

Do your research

You need to research the publication and the journalist that you are pitching to. When you contact a journalist demonstrate your knowledge of the publication or discuss some of the articles previously written by the journalist. Journalists will be more likely to use your pitch when it is specifically tailored to their publication.

Email your pitch

Journalists prefer to receive emails so contact them via email first, then conduct a follow-up phone call two days later.

Pitch with intention

Be very specific when you send a pitch. Journalists like it when you send them a pitch that details exactly what section of the publication your information would be perfect for.

Put the reader first

Put yourself in the reader's shoes and communicate to them.

Create a relationship with a journalist

Journalists receive hundreds of emails a day and don't have time to look at every email. If you have a relationship with a journalist then they are more likely to read your emails because they already know you.

Be friendly but not overly familiar

For example never call a journalist 'honey' or give them a nickname if you don't have a great relationship with them.

1st person or 3rd person?

If you are doing your own PR, either write your pitch in 3rd person and send it from an email address that isn't your own. (Maybe start an email address that is your fictitious PR person!) If you are sending it from your email address, then make sure your pitch is in first person. Both work, equally as well.

Media Pitch Template

Email subject line: Potential story idea: XYZ [Succinctly outline your topic]

Hi [always address a journalist with their correctly spelt first name]

{Paragraph 1}

- I thought you might be interested in an interview with me, I am an expert in ...
- Outline the topic, issue, problem or point of interest. This needs to be succinct and attention grabbing so a journalist can quickly read what the pitch is about.
- For instance, 'why MBAs can sometimes be overrated'.

{Paragraph 2-3}

- Explain why this issue, problem or point of interest is important, interesting and newsworthy.
- For instance, 'When considering postgraduate study, many aspiring business leaders and CEOs question whether to undertake a MBA or a Masters Degree.

{Paragraph 3-5}

- Explain why you can comment on this. For an issue you can explain what the solution could be. This is related to the expert's business i.e. product or service and how it can solve the problem.
- For instance, 'I can discuss why a specialist Masters Degree can, in many cases, be of more value than a MBA, which tend to be more general.

I have extensive experience in both types of postgraduate study. I have been involved for many years with the University of Technology, Sydney's MBA program as Head of the School of Management, studied a Masters degree at the Macquarie Graduate School of Management and am Director of Graduate Studies at Macquarie University's Faculty of Business and Economics.'

{Paragraph 6}

- You may also want to consider outlining key topics or points you can make.

- For instance, 'I can discuss:
  - The difference between a 'generalist' and 'specialist' Masters Degree.
  - Why the choice of program must take into consideration which undergraduate degree you have studied and the career path you aspire to.

{Paragraph 7}

Please let me know if this is of interest and if you would like an interview.

Regards

Examples of pitches:

1st person

Media: Marketing Magazine

Subject: Potential story topic: How SMEs can use social media and PR innovatively.

Hi ##

I thought you may be interested in an interview with me regarding expert comment on the collaboration of public relations and digital media for SMEs with a focus on social media.

Most of my clients are SMEs and being a small business owner myself, I have used the combination of PR and digital marketing to significantly raise the profile of my clients (as well as myself).

SMEs can often feel as though it's impossible to compete with huge companies but when it comes to social media SMEs have got the edge as they have more opportunity to 'show the human side' to their business.

The key to social media, whether it be blogs, Facebook, Twitter, YouTube or LinkedIn, is to break down the barriers between a logo and a consumer; to reveal the people behind the brand. For big companies with various levels of management and lots of red tape, it can be difficult to honestly show this side of the company yet for small and medium businesses, it's easy for them to appear accessible to their customers.

By combining traditional PR with digital, SMEs have the opportunity to reach a much wider audience and make more of an impact with their messages.

I would be happy to discuss the collaboration of PR and social media for SMEs and offer insight into some of the best ways to use the two to advance a business.

If you are interested in an interview please contact me on the details below. I look forward to hearing from you.

Kind regards,

Catriona

3rd person

Media: The Australian

Subject: Potential story topic: Are reconciliation plans just lip service?

Hi ##

I thought you might be interested in an interview with Ros Moriarty, Managing Director of Jumbana Group, on why many company reconciliation plans don't achieve anything.

Since Prime Minister Kevin Rudd formerly apologised to the stolen generations in 2008, it has become a common practice for larger organisations to produce reconciliation plans. However, there is a question as to how many are fulfilling their plans.

Ros can discuss why for many organisations a reconciliation plan has become another governance box to tick, particularly for publically listed companies whose annual report is scrutinised by the public.

She can explain while having a reconciliation plan is a great first step there's still work to be done to promote diverse and inclusive workforces in Australia.

Ros can discuss some of the work Indigenous company Jumbana Group is doing with its clients to put reconciliation plans in action, like supplier diversity initiatives and workplace training.

Please let me know if this is of interest and if I can arrange an interview with Ros. It may also be possible to interview a client of Jumbana Group to discuss their reconciliation plans.

Develop two Story Angles & Pitches

Knowing how to pitch a story idea is critical to achieving media coverage, so take action and develop two story angles and pitches.

ACTION STEP

Visit **www.UnknownToExpertBonus.com**
For Your FREE Bonus Action Step Content

ACCELERATE YOUR OUTCOME

Additional **Media Pitch Examples** (that I personally used to generate over a million dollars in media exposure) and other valuable content to accelerate your journey from Unknown To Expert available at:
www.UnknownToExpertFaster.com

VALUE: $2000 ONLY $97

How to pitch to radio

Radio programs usually have a specific audience of listeners, which allows you to communicate directly to your customers, clients or a niche group of people.

Pitching to radio is different than pitching to TV or print media because the news cycle is quicker, they have various segments and the journalists have different roles.

Here are some tips to help you pitch to radio:

Have a newsworthy story

To be featured in a radio interview you need to have something newsworthy or interesting you can discuss. Maybe you are an expert on a topic that is currently in the news or maybe you're doing something really exciting a journalist would be interested in. Your topic must appeal to the program's target audience and conform to the topics they usually discuss.

Know the segments

Do some research into the radio programs your target audiences listen to and get to know more about them. Some radio stations have specific segments you can pitch to. For example there may be a segment related to your topic of expertise.

Most radio stations have breakfast, morning, afternoon and drive shows. So if your story is related, these segments are a good place to pitch to.

Who to pitch to

You need to find out who the best person is to pitch your story to. In most cases this will be the program producer rather than the host of the show, as they are involved in planning the show's content.

If you don't have access to a media database you can find out who to pitch to by calling the radio station's switchboard and asking for the name and contact details of a specific segment producer.

How to pitch

In most cases, it's better to pitch to a radio producer with a phone call rather than an email. Radio journalists tend to work at a very fast pace and your email may be lost.

When pitching to a journalist you need to explain why you would be a great person to interview. You also need to explain why your interview would be of interest to the program's listeners.

When doing phone pitches, make sure you practice beforehand and write down what you are going to say. You have a better chance of success if you appear confident, knowledgeable and get your point across quickly. If you stumble for words and don't know what you are going to say, a journalist may lose interest.

Pitch at the right time

Timing is everything. If you catch a journalist at the wrong time they will be unlikely to listen to your pitch. Never call a radio journalist or producer during a live broadcast or while they are on air (unless it's talkback). They will be too busy at this time and you will just annoy them.

Know what times the radio program airs and make your call before or shortly after the broadcast ends.

Here is an example of a pitch to radio:

Media: Mainstream new/social affairs

Subject: Interview opportunity: John Moriarty – Australia Day does not demean Indigenous history & heritage

Hi ##

I thought you might be interested in an interview with John Moriarty, a member of the Yanyuwa people from NT and Chairman of Indigenous art and consulting company, The Jumbana Group, on why Australia Day does not demean Indigenous history and heritage.

Part of the stolen generation, John's view is not one of sadness or anger thinking of Australia Day as Invasion Day. Instead John sees the Day as a great celebration of all things Australian, including Indigenous culture.

John believes reconciliation needs to be a two-way street so as a united country we can move forward, forgive old hurts and build a new contemporary national identity. Positive action is what is needed to heal and put Indigenous Australians on an even playing field.

John has always been passionate about the plight of Indigenous peoples in Australia. He has held numerous positions in Indigenous affairs, such as a board member for the National Indigenous Advisory Committee to SOCOG, the Sydney Harbour Federation Trust, the National Indigenous Council, the National Aboriginal and Islander Health Council, the Australia International Cultural Committee, plus many others.

One of John's current projects is not-for-profit initiative John Moriarty Football (JMF). As the first Aboriginal to be selected to play soccer for Australia, John sees the impact that sport can bring to children's lives. JMF is a program for under six, eight and ten year olds uses football (soccer) to improve school attendance and achieve sustainable, healthier outcomes for families and communities.

Please let me know if this is of interest and if I can arrange an interview with John.

Write your Radio Pitch

18

Now it's time to write your radio pitch.
Open your Action Step and start now.

ACTION STEP

Visit **www.UnknownToExpertBonus.com**
For Your FREE Bonus Action Step Content

How to pitch to TV

What do television producers specifically look for in a pitch? An idea that works brilliantly for print may never get picked up by TV and may leave you scratching your head as to why.

Here is some advice on pitching to TV producers:

Visuals, visuals, visuals

Regardless of whether it's the evening news, a morning show or a current affairs program, if you want your story to get on TV you need to put some thought into the visuals.

Make it easy for the producer to say yes by suggesting a few different visuals they could use in relation to the story you're pitching. This creates less work for them and more chance of success for you!

Keep it topical

If you're aiming at news programs, a strong news angle will be required. Even if you're pitching to a morning show or current affairs program, you will have the best success if you link your pitch to something topical. If the producers can relate your idea to a current story in the media it gives them more incentive to run with the idea.

Case studies and interviews

Real people add real interest. Rather than offering dry information or statistics, try to provide an interesting case study and suggest some related visuals to go with the interview. Provide the producer with a rundown on your background and involvement, the juicier the better.

Be direct with your pitch

There is no time for beating around the bush. A producer will usually just skim the first few sentences of the hundreds of emails they receive daily so you want your pitch to stand out. Don't wait until the third paragraph to get to the point.

News or promotion?

TV producers won't be interested if you're just pushing a product without a good hook. Your product/service should take a back seat to the actual story. Keep in mind that any mention of your product/service is valuable but it is the story that will get you TV coverage. A good tip is to clearly state why the story you are offering is topical but different to others that have been run recently.

If you're pitching to a storytelling show like a morning show or A Current Affair, try offering them a clear beginning, middle and end to your story as their audiences appreciate a contained and interesting package.

Here is an example of a pitch to television:

Hi (name),

We thought (TV Show name) might be interested in an interview opportunity with Andrew Griffiths. Andrew is an internationally renowned personal development writer and Australia's number one business expert.

Andrew Griffiths has led a very interesting life. He is an entrepreneur with a real passion for business, but he came from humble beginnings. He grew up in a violent and neglectful home, was abandoned by his parents and does not know when or where he was born.

Since then Andrew has turned his life around. He has written nine hugely successful books, with many more on the way. His "101 Ways" business building series offers small business owners practical, smart and realistic advice. He has also recently published the inspirational The Me Myth, a personal development book encouraging readers to look at life differently. His books are now sold in over 50 countries around the world, in places as far away as Estonia, Nigeria, China and even Iceland.

Some interview concepts that Andrew can speak about using topics from his The Me Myth book include:

What do you mean it's not all about me? We live in a world where we are bombarded with messages telling us that the world actually does revolve around us. As we all search for a more meaningful and rewarding life, the concept that perhaps it doesn't is sometimes tough for people to grasp. But if you embrace the habit of looking outwards instead of inwards, your entire life will change for the better.

We've all had to deal with challenges in the past, some worse than others. The reality is these challenges shouldn't shape the rest of our lives but sadly too many people do. The point is that where we come from doesn't matter, where we are going does. Stop making excuses about the past and get out there and build the life you want.

Intuition is a sense that is just as valid as sight, smell and touch. But we go through life listening to this sense less and less. Intuition is a sense that has evolved over hundreds of thousands of years to help us survive, to protect us and to make our life safer. Why on earth wouldn't we listen to it more? So how do you tune into your intuition?

You hate your life and your job. Stop complaining and make some positive changes. Andrew will outline steps how to make positive changes, regardless of where you are and the challenges that you are facing.

Please let me know if you would like any further information or would like to arrange an interview with Andrew Griffiths.

Write Your TV Pitch

Now it's time to write your TV pitch.
Jump over to your Action Step to draft your pitch.

Visit **www.UnknownToExpertBonus.com**
For Your FREE Bonus Action Step Content

Tactic 3: Contributed articles

Articles are a fantastic way of getting publicity, but they have to be written in a specific way.

Many publications welcome well written articles on topics of interest to their readers. However, they should never be a blatant advertisement or advertorial.

You can write an article that positions you as an industry expert and offers topical, helpful information. Before starting, think about what the readers of the publication you will be pitching it to are interested in.

Be objective

Journalists are more interested in articles that provide valuable information to their readers than promotional pieces about your business. When writing an article you need to remain objective and avoid writing in the first person, for instance don't use the phrases 'I think' and 'my opinion'. Write the article in an informative and entertaining manner and stay on topic.

Know the audience

Before writing the article, think about the audience of the publication that will be reading it. Make sure the article is about a topic that would interest them and try to provide valuable, helpful information. Another good point is to avoid using industry specific jargon if your audience has no knowledge of your industry.

Topic

Topics can include: identify a problem and give a solution, suggest a new approach, describe the lessons learnt from a project and their applications to other areas or even how to do aspects of your business.

I have found 'How to" articles to be the most effective. For example, I regularly write articles on topics related to my business such as "how to write a media release", "how to develop a PR campaign" and even "how to write an article"!

It is essential the article is written in an objective, informative and entertaining manner. You will be wasting your time (and the editor's) if you write anything off topic or promotional.

Get a copy of the publication you want to send the article to and see what type of articles they print and their style. For example, a medical journal will expect very technical information, but a magazine about knitting will want tips, techniques and photos of your knitting projects.

Editorial guidelines

Most publications have editorial guidelines and it is important to take a look at these before sending in an article. For example, the magazine *Working Women*, published by Women's Network Australia, is looking for articles that help their readers in their personal and business lives. Over 65 percent of Women's Network Australia members run their own businesses, so an article on tips, strategies and techniques that assist in running a business is what the editor wants to see.

Photos

Many publications like to publish photos of the article author. If they request a photo, don't send a happy snap from your family album. Submit a professional and high resolution photo, and by doing this your story will have more of a chance of getting a run.

Other key points include:

- The length of the article. Find out the number of words the editor is looking for and keep within the word count. You will have a much better chance of getting published.
- The deadline. Every publication runs to editorial and advertising deadlines and it is essential you submit the article before the deadline.
- Write in short clear sentences, using sub headings and dot points, and bolding to communicate key points.
- Articles are invariably improved by allowing a few days to go by

and then returning to your work.

- Proof read your article and even ask someone else to check it before sending it to the publication. Other people see things you don't and their final finesse can turn your article from good to great.

How to pitch an article to the media

When pitching an article to a publication, the aim of the pitch is to succinctly explain why the article is relevant and of value to the publication's readers.

Many publications – especially online publications – are starved for content and are more than happy to take a readymade article to publish (as long as the content is of value to their target audience).

Pitching an article on how to grow carrots to a publication such as *Business Review Australia* just isn't going to be accepted, so it is vital that you research and understand exactly what type of content the publication will and won't want.

There are two ways to pitch an article:

1. You can proactively pitch an article to a publication knowing that the article is within their guidelines and based on a topic their readers will find interesting and of value.

2. You can pitch an article in regards to an upcoming feature or special edition as contributed content for that specific feature.

Article pitch template - Here is the step-by-step process of how to draft a pitch for an article:

1. Start a pitch for an article with: "We thought that you might be interested in an article on <topic of article> for <name of publication and, if possible, suggest the section within the publication you think it could be suitable for>."
2. The pitch should provide an overview/angle of the article and emphasise why the article is appropriate to be published in the publication.
3. When writing a pitch for an article, briefly outline the main or most interesting points of the article. This will allow the journalist to get an

idea of what the article is going to be about.

4. Ensure that the angle of the pitch is relevant for the publication.

5. The final sentence of the pitch should read: "I hope that you find this article interesting. Please find the article attached and do not hesitate to contact us if you need further information."

6. Always send the article as a Word document – not a PDF as they can't copy words from a PDF.

Here is an example of a pitch for an article:

Hi #,

I thought you might be interested in the attached article I have written about How to generate quality content for your marketing campaign. I am Chief Marketing Officer of XYZ, a global marketing software company.

The article was written with internet retailers in mind, explaining how they can take advantage of the trend of buyers researching products and services online. Internet retailers can take this opportunity to provide useful, accessible information so that consumers research and purchase in the same place.

The article provides four steps to creating and managing content that will drive sales, by making information about your product or service accessible in many locations and that meets the needs of buyers.

I am a 25-year marketing veteran and global thought leader. My article has been written with your audience in mind and is technical yet easy to read.

Please let me know if you would like more information or would like to use the article.

Drafting Your Article Pitch

It's so fantastic to open a magazine or web page and see your very own article printed. So take action and write an amazing pitch and make it happen.

Visit **www.UnknownToExpertBonus.com**
For Your FREE Bonus Action Step Content

Features lists

Many publications like to plan out the topics that they will be focusing on for each issue – in addition to their regular sections. These topics are called features, and are used mainly to attract advertising agencies and organisations to advertise in their publication if the feature topic fits with their business.

Features generally take up anything from two to six pages in a publication, so they are a great tool for businesses and individuals to take advantage of to gain exposure with their target audiences.

A features list is a calendar of editorial and advertising content coming up in the next six months to a year for a publication, and it's a great indication of what they really want to focus on when it comes to articles and interview topics.

Although features lists can be subject to change and not all publications will have one, the majority of those that do will usually stick to what has been planned. This means, once you find your key publications' features lists you will have a six month to a year plan of where you can pitch angles and articles in regards to upcoming features.

This doesn't mean you stop proactively pitching angles and articles – features is just another strategy you can use to gain the journalists' attention, get your story in the media and start creating relationships.

Features for magazines and newspapers can generally be found in their media kits, located on the publication's advertising section of its website.

Sometimes finding the media kit can be straightforward, and other times it can take a bit of digging around the website.

Some media kits still won't have a features list, in which case you may have to email the sales or advertising team to request one. Don't be afraid to ask for one. If they don't have a features list, they will let you know and if they do, they should be happy to send you through a copy.

Find Key Features for Your Key Publications

21

ACTION STEP

Map out the next three months of suitable features and take action to find features for your key publications – and then pitch to them.

Visit **www.UnknownToExpertBonus.com**
For Your FREE Bonus Action Step Content

How to pitch for features

When sending a pitch for a feature, ensure that it does not come across as though you are trying to sell something. Rather, outline the great story that you have to tell the journalist and why it is relevant for the feature.

1. Start the pitch with the sentence: "I noticed that you have a feature on <proposed features topic> coming up in <name of publication> and I wanted to give you information on <your name and what you do>.

2. Outline what you have to offer the journalist for their story. Include a sentence such as "I would love to have a chat with you about...."

3. Always end a pitch with the sentence: "Please let me know if you would like to arrange an interview or need further information. I look forward to hearing from you."

4. Paste it in an email and write in the subject line of the email "Media Information for *<name of upcoming feature>* feature coming up in # magazine".

Here is an example of a pitch for a feature:

Hi #,

I noticed you have a 'Digital' feature coming up and thought you would be interested in speaking with me about best practice digital marketing and how digital agencies can provide a much more beneficial service than in-house.

I am CEO of XYZ, a digital marketing agency with more than 15 years experience in the digital marketing space and is a leader in creating successful digital strategies for clients throughout the Asia-Pacific region.

When it comes to outsourcing, choosing a digital agency for one small service may not be the best course of action. Organisations may hire a digital agency just for web development, but what if web development isn't what the organisation really needs? I can discuss how creating partnerships and hiring agencies across multiple digital services can be more beneficial for an organisation as a digital agency then has the ability to pinpoint what exactly is not working.

I can also discuss how factors, such as absolute control and being able to leverage singular resources with wide range of skill sets, make the internal approach seem the more attractive option, however, once you drill down a bit further and consider benefits of a digital agency approach, such as their breadth of experience, scalability, redundancy, the cost savings and leveraging relevant experience, the internal option seems to lose its appeal.

If you would like to speak to me or if you have any other questions please let me know.

Regards,

#

Draft a Pitch for An Upcoming Feature

Draft a pitch for an upcoming feature.
Open your Action Step and start now.

ACTION STEP

Visit **www.UnknownToExpertBonus.com**
For Your FREE Bonus Action Step Content

Other places to find story opportunities

Besides proactive pitching and looking at upcoming features for publications, there are a few other places you can look for media coverage opportunities:

Source media service

Most countries have a service that connects journalists and sources or spokespeople.

In Australia it's called SourceBottle which is a free online service and sends out an e-newsletter twice a day which lists a whole range of journalist call outs for spokespeople on different topics.

It is completely free and very easy to sign up to, plus it allows you to pick and choose the topics you are most interested in receiving call outs about.

You can then pitch yourself in to the opportunities of interest via the Source Bottle website.

Register for SourceBottle here: www.sourcebottle.com.au.

In the US it's called HARO and you can register here: www.helpareporter.com

Twitter

If you are on Twitter ensure you are following the journalists and editors of your key publications. Many of them will turn to Twitter to ask their followers for spokespeople to provide comments on a particular story they are working on.

To make this a bit easier, create a list on your Twitter account that only includes the journalists and editors you are following. This list will ensure you aren't missing any important tweets from journalists in your main stream.

Topical news

If there is an upcoming event or launch that has relevance to your area of expertise, or if something happens in the media that you feel you could comment on, use the opportunity to pitch to the journalist writing the story to offer expert commentary.

For example, if your expertise is about the future of mobile technology, you can pitch yourself into a technology publication or even the technology section of a newspaper as an expert to comment on the latest iPhone launch to discuss its features.

Media lists

A media list documents the key media contacts in your industry who would be interested in your story angles. These contacts can include journalists, producers, bloggers, freelancers and editors.

Here is a step-by-step guide to creating a media list:

Find your audience

The purpose of a media list is to gain coverage in publications that your target audiences use or view. This means you need to write a list of all the publications (online and offline), blogs, TV and radio programs that appeal to your target audiences.

Identify contacts

Once you have a list of media outlets, you now need to identify the appropriate contact person to send your information to. Usually the most appropriate contact is the reporter or editor who covers the topic in your media release or pitch.

You can find their email address or phone number on the media outlet's website or call them directly. Try to avoid sending your media release to the email address for general enquiries or 'news@' because it usually will not reach the right contact person in that publication.

Create a database

Organise your media list into a database, such as Excel, with separate columns for the name of the publication, the contact person, their job title, email address and phone number.

	First Name	Last Name	Position	Publication	Email	Phone
1	First Name	Last Name	Position	Publication	Email	Phone
2	**Marketing and Media**					
3	Gary	Tay	Online Editor	Adoi Magazine	gary-v@doimagazine.com	6016-376 261
4	Allein	Moore	Editor	AdAsia	editor@adasia.com.sg	N/A
5	Matthew	Miller	Online Editor	Campaign Asia	matthew.miller@haymarket.asia	852 3175 1502
6	Magz	Osbourne	Sout East Asia Editor	Campaign Asia	magz.osborne@haymarket.asia	55 6179 0051
7	Andrew	Woodward	Managing Editor	Campaign Asia	andrew.woodward@haymarket.asia	852 3175 1966
8	Kim	Shaw	Editor	Campaign Brief Asia	kim@campaignbrief.com	61 437 920 344
9	Abby	Yao	Associate Editor	Adobo Magazine	editorial@adobomagazine.com	132 045 0218
10	Clive	Gulliver	Editor	Asia Pulse International	cgulliver@asia.com.au	02 9002 0800
11				Asia Media	asiamedia@international.ucla.edu	
12	Adaline	Lau	Editor	ClickZ.Asia	via website	N/A
13	**Business & Finance**					
14				Asia Week magazine	mail@web.asiaweek.com	
15	Chaitanya	Kalbag	Editor	Business Today	c.kalbag@intoday.com	
16	Jame	DiBiasio	Editor	Asian Investor	jame.dibiasio@haymarket.asia	852 2122 5207
17				Asian Business	editor@asianbusiness.com.hk	n/a
18	Lara	Wozniak	Editor	Finance Asia	lara.wozniak@financeasia.com	852 3121 5255
19	Richard	Morrow	Editor	Asia money	richard.morrow@asiamoney.com	852 2126 4024
20	Lorraine	Cuchnie	Online Editor	Asia money	lorraine.cuchnie@asiamoney.com	123 2253 8875
21				Capital Magazine	editor@capmagazine.asia	N/A
22	James	Elva	Editor	Brand Equity	james.elva@brandequity.com.my	876 21 3 2065
23	Perry	Tan	Editor	CRM Management	perry@questexasia.com	N/A
24	Joseph	Rebeiro	Editor	SMB World Asia	jrebeiro@questexasia.com	N/A
25	Cesar	Bacani	Editor-in-Chief	CFO Innovation	cesar.bacani@questexasia.com	N/A
26	Angie	Mak	Online Editor	CFO Innovation	amak@questexasia.com	N/A
27	Teng	Fang Yhi	Editor	MIS Asia	teng.fangyhi@questexasia.com	N/A

This is what an Excel media database can look like. Use these spreadsheets to organise and categorise your media lists.

Categorise your list

You should categorise your list into different sections for each media outlet. For example, you could create a section for all your newspaper contacts and another section for all your magazine contacts. A better way to categorise your list is by topics or areas of interest.

Update your list regularly

Media professionals often change their career or areas of expertise, which means you should constantly update your media list. Remember to update your list if your contact person changes or if you find new contacts.

If creating your own media list sounds too hard then you can get help from an online media guide such as Margaret Gee's Australian Media Guide or AAP Media Net Media Database. These sites provide an online database of contact information for media professionals.

Another alternative is to hire a PR agency because they have an extensive list of media contacts and know how to create a perfect media list.

Once you have created your media list you can start contacting journalists to gain media coverage in the most appropriate media to reach your target audience.

Approximate lead times

Newspapers	Being put to bed	Developing stories
Newspapers (general news section)	The day before	3-4 days before
Newspaper sections e.g. My Career, Media, Drive, TV Guide etc.	2 weeks before	4-8 weeks before
Newspaper colour magazine supplements	4 weeks before	9-12 weeks before

Magazines	Being put to bed	Developing stories
Glossy monthly women's magazines	3 months before	5 months before
Other monthly magazines	3 months before	4 months before
Monthly trade or industry magazines	1 month before	2-3 months before
Weekly magazines e.g. WHO, Woman's Day	1 month before	9-12 weeks before
Weekly business magazines	1-3 weeks before	2 months before

Create a Media List

Now it's time to create a media list.
Jump over to your Action Step to start now.

Visit **www.UnknownToExpertBonus.com**
For Your FREE Bonus Action Step Content

Additional **Media Lists, including Australian Blogs and Media Outlets and Media List Template** and other valuable content to accelerate your journey from Unknown To Expert available at:
www.UnknownToExpertFaster.com

VALUE: $2000
ONLY
$97

Following up the media

So you've sent out a pitch or a media release to journalists and have received no reply. What now? What should you do to find out if the journalist received your email or if they are interested? An essential skill to conduct successful media relations is to learn how to follow up with the media over the phone.

The best way to follow up with a journalist is by calling them. An appropriate time to follow up is usually two to three days after the email pitch or media release has been sent. Never wait more than a week to follow up as waiting too long may result in the journalist deleting your email, the story being covered by another person or the story becoming (quite literally) yesterday's news.

When it comes to following up journalists, the best advice would be to go with your gut instinct – listen to their tone of voice and the way they phrase their answers and make decisions based on that.

Sometimes that can be a bit hard to do, so here are a few tips you should always take into account when following up with a journalist:

Prepare

One way to calm your nerves and sound more confident on the phone is to plan out what you want to get across – your pitch or key points. Any phone conversation, however, can be unpredictable, especially when dealing with a journalist. The best way to tackle any response from a journalist is to be flexible and prepared for anything. You may need to resend the media release or answer detailed questions on the spot. More than likely you will need to leave a voice message, so be prepared for that.

Be specific

Be very specific about the media pitch or media release you sent them. Don't just say "I sent you a media release and wanted to know if you were interested".

Be polite and speak clearly

When calling a journalist speak clearly and be very direct and to the point. Try to sound interested and enthusiastic to make the call interesting for the journalist.

Don't be afraid of journalists

Don't be intimidated by journalists, they are people too. If you contact them at a bad time apologise once and move on. Apologising more than that is unnecessary and can be annoying.

Choose your questions wisely

When calling a journalist don't ask them if they are going to publish the media release. Instead, tell them the date you sent the media release and what it was regarding. Simply ask if they received the media release and if they would like further information or high resolution images.

Be ready to respond to their requests

You should be ready to supply the journalist with relevant images and additional information. You can also line up an interview for the journalist to make it easier for them to cover your story.

Remember, after every follow up to make a note of the outcome to ensure you remember who you have called and who was interested.

The most important thing to remember when conducting a media follow up is to remain confident and try to provide the most appropriate and interesting information for the journalist. With a little bit of preparation beforehand, you can then hang up the phone feeling like you've achieved your goal and confident you've maintained a good relationship with the journalist.

Here is a basic template for a phone follow up:

"Hi, this is # (your name).

"I sent you a media release/media angle/article/case study on (date) regarding (topic). I am just checking that you received it and…

For a media release: If you would you like any additional information or images?"

For an article/case study: If you were interested in using the article/case study in (publication name)?"

For a media pitch: If it would be something your readers would be interested in?"

Journalists are very busy and won't always be available to take your call. If they do, it doesn't automatically mean they will know what email you are talking about. Here are a couple of possible scenarios and what to say:

Scenario 1

Journalist: Yes, I read it and it's interesting – tell me more about it.

What to say: Outline the key points (messages) from media release/ media angle/article/case study.

Scenario 2 – The answering machine comes on.

What to say: Say exactly the same thing as above, speak clearly and leave your email address and phone number. Spell out your email address if you have to.

Scenario 3

Journalist: I am not looking after that media release, my colleague is. I will forward it to them.

What to say: Is it ok if I can get their name and email address because I'm happy to forward it to them? Tip: Also try to get their direct line.

Scenario 4

Journalist: I haven't even looked at that media release yet.

What to say: When do you think you'll be looking at it? Tip: Note down the date and send through the information again closer to the date.

Scenario 5

Journalist: I don't remember receiving that, could you send it through again?

What to say: No problem, I'll send it through right now.

Your Follow Up Script

Before you do a phone follow up, draft a script following the template. Jump over to the Action Step to draft your script.

ACTION STEP

Visit **www.UnknownToExpertBonus.com**
For Your FREE Bonus Action Step Content

ACCELERATE YOUR OUTCOME

Additional **Phone Follow Template** and other valuable content to accelerate your journey from Unknown To Expert available at:

www.UnknownToExpertFaster.com

Media interviews

Your pitch was successful and the journalist has agreed to interview you. So how can you make the most of this opportunity and come out of it shining?

Each medium – radio, TV and print – have specific requirements you should understand before the interview.

Radio

The main feature of radio is that it is a personal medium. Radio gives the illusion of a one-to-one relationship, which means that you should adopt an appropriate style when you go on radio programs.

You should adopt a friendly approach in interviews on programs such as talkback. In radio you are talking to or with people, not at them.

Radio is not the medium for complex explanations or lists of facts and statistics. The listeners have to be able to grasp your point quickly and easily as there is no visual reinforcement and no hard copy to check back for verifications.

Before your radio interview, find out whether the interview will be live or pre-recorded. A pre-recorded interview can often be edited, whereas a live interview cannot.

Television

Television is demanding in the sense that the audience sees you as well as hears you. Your body language, dress, background and movement all contribute to communication with the audience.

To appear credible on television, you must sound and look credible. Sit rather than stand and remember to use slow, controlled gestures. Review your appearance before the interview, ensuring your dress, hair and facial expressions come across as credible.

The power of television is its visual impact; you must be brief, to the point and get the key message across in a limited time. Allow yourself time to think about the question and use silence instead of filler words, such as 'um', while thinking.

Find out when you need to arrive and whether you must wear or bring anything in particular.

Print/online

Press interviews have similar requirements as electronic media in terms of news value and brevity.

The apparent relaxed nature of press interviews should not lull you into a false sense of security. Ensure you get your key messages in early, be careful not to ramble and place tonal emphasis on key points. A trick for press interviews over the phone is to stand up while doing the interview - it will give you a lot more confidence.

Find out whether the interview will be in person, over the phone, or via email. Ask if they need a high resolution (300dpi/1mb in size or more) head shot of yourself or any other images.

Pointers for interview preparation

- Ask them what they are focusing on in the feature (if related to a feature pitch) or what type of information they need.
- Ask them their deadline and when it is most convenient for them to interview you.
- Make sure you call them at the agreed time.
- Do not ask the journalist to see the questions or the story in advance – not only will the answer be 'no' but it could be detrimental to your relationship with the journalist.
- Remember, you cannot change your quotes or edit the story after the interview. More often than not, the journalist will be interviewing other people to ensure the story has a balanced view, so do not expect to be the only person interviewed or quoted.
- Before you undertake the interview you will need to write out a game plan. You should prepare one before each and every interview.

The game plan covers key issues, possible questions about the key issues and the answers for each possible question.

- It is important to write the game plan out - don't do it from memory. If you are doing a phone interview, have the plan in front you for easy reference.

- Develop compelling messages: What are the critical messages that you want to communicate? Key messages are the core messages you want your audience to hear and remember. They create meaning, headline the issue and allow you to control the interview.

- With your audience in mind, and focused on your objectives, you should work out in advance of the interview what you must say on the topic concerned.

- The journalist's role is not to try to catch you out (unless it's A Current Affair!), but to establish the facts and report on them objectively. If you focus on waiting for them to ask a tricky question, you will not be in control of the interview.

- Journalists are looking for the truth. If you try to get a story by making claims that cannot be substantiated, it will not lead to a story. The article will not be published and they will certainly never ask you for an interview again.

- Ensure that any information you provide the journalist, such as statistics, can be substantiated.

- Try to develop an understanding of the audience the journalist will be writing for so you can set your agenda accordingly. It is worth looking up the journalist's publication on the internet or buying a copy. If you have time, read some articles they have written so you can understand their style.

- Practice your answers and your key messages to ensure you have a sound knowledge of what you want to say.

Blogger outreach

Effective blogs have a dedicated readership and a high Google ranking, so it's a great PR opportunity. They are an interesting alternative to traditional news sources.

Research

Find out who the major bloggers on the topic are, what their specific area of interest is and whether they accept media releases or guest blogging. The more information they provide about themselves, the better. If their contact information isn't provided, they probably don't want to be contacted.

Read the blog to see if it is a good fit for your expertise, and choose carefully who you would like to be associated with. Keep track of your information in a spreadsheet, as you would for a media list, and make a note of any interaction you have with the blogger.

The most time consuming part of blogger outreach is research, but give it the time it requires and you will see results. (Refer to section three for more details on how to identify the right bloggers for you.)

How to approach bloggers

Bloggers should not be approached in the same way you approach a journalist. Most bloggers are writing about the topics they are passionate about – they don't need people pitching media angles, articles or products and services to them. Approaching a blogger has to be much more personal and be very, very targeted.

Sending an irrelevant media release to them is obviously a big no-no. Rather than pitching a general media release, be sure to make your contact with the blogger a little more personal than you would with a journalist.

Read their blog first, make mention of posts that interested you and if possible make this friendly contact before sending a 'pitch' email. You can also start building a relationship with relevant bloggers by posting comments on their blog and engaging with them.

Bloggers won't always publish a phone number on their site so a follow up phone call is not always possible which is why building the relationship first will usually deliver more promising results than a one-off email pitch. When a relationship has been built, a blogger will generally be more receptive to your ideas.

The pitch should be in the form of an email – which needs to be clear and to the point. Busy people do not read long emails, so in the first paragraph clearly outline your idea. Always start by introducing yourself, explain your area of expertise and why you think it is a good match for their blog.

Never be pushy, and always ask if they are happy to be contacted about story angles. Clarify with them that they don't have to write about it – if they like it they can write about it.

What do you pitch?

Bloggers usually won't publish obvious advertising material. Pitch engaging, relevant content that will appeal to their readers. Consider pitching an interview or story opportunity of interest to their readership.

Blogger outreach comes back to two things: relevant and compelling content, and relationships. Give it the time it needs and be ready to give up control of the message – bloggers will write whatever they want to.

Blogger pitch template

Start a pitch with: "I've been reading your blog <name> and I found <post> interesting for <reason>.

The pitch should offer your post/angle and emphasise why the post is appropriate for this blog. Be friendly.

Briefly outline the main or most interesting points of the post/idea. This will allow the blogger to get an idea of what the article is going to be about.

Ensure that the angle of the pitch is relevant for the blog.

The final sentence of the pitch should read: "I hope that you find this interesting. Please find the post attached and do not hesitate to contact us if you need further information."

Here is an example of a blogger pitch:

Subject: Career advice for professional women

Hi ##,

I really love reading Leaders in Heels, especially your Q&As with successful women in business. It can be difficult for female business owners to find role models and inspiration and your site is a great place for them to get the advice and inspiration they may need during challenging times.

As a platform that aims to inspire women I thought Leaders in Heels may be interested in expert advice to professional women to help them develop skills for success.

I founded my marketing agency when I was only 23 years old and independently grew it to be an award-winning player in the marketing industry. I am a past Telstra Young Business Woman of the Year and love to share my experience and learnings with other women who would like to venture out on their own. Here are some of my tips.

Advice #1

Self-evaluate. Knowing your strengths will help you to better communicate them to prospective and current employers when job hunting or asking for that promotion or pay rise. It also helps you find those areas of opportunity and to work on them.

Advice #2

Be genuine in everything you do, both in and outside of work. Humility, admitting failure and genuinely being curious in every conversation you have, will be recognised and appreciated. This isn't a common personality trait, especially at work, so you will stand out. Please contact us on ## if you would like more information or if you would like to use these tips.

Blogger Pitch

25 ACTION STEP

Now it's time to pitch to bloggers. Many bloggers love to receive new material from experts in their field, so take action and pitch to three bloggers you have found.

Visit **www.UnknownToExpertBonus.com**
For Your FREE Bonus Action Step Content

ACCELERATE YOUR OUTCOME

Additional **Blogger Pitch Template** (that I personally used to generate over a million dollars in media exposure) and other valuable content to accelerate your journey from Unknown To Expert available at:
www.UnknownToExpertFaster.com

VALUE: $2000
ONLY
$97

Own the Light

At Star 5 you will see that through social media you can own the light. Now you are your own media platform where you control your brand, stories and content.

Social media is a critical step in developing your profile as a thought leader and expert. It is an essential communication tool as it allows you to communicate directly with your audiences - unfiltered by anyone else, including media.

When you are pitching stories to the media, they decide what gets published and they filter your stories and messages. With social media, you decide. You tell the stories that help your branding the most and you know are most valuable to your audiences.

So why do social media? The obvious answer is, the more people that know about you, the more chances you have of landing a new business opportunity, speaking gig or promotion.

It's all about relationships. With social media, you are developing credible relationships with huge numbers of people directly – often they feel that this relationship is one-on-one as you are providing valuable information and engaging them in conversations.

As you travel through this section I challenge you to think of yourself as a media broadcaster. You choose your messages and your platforms. You own the light.

Now there are so many platforms to choose from: Facebook, Twitter, podcasting, Slideshare, Instagram, YouTube, Pinterest, LinkedIn, Google+ and so many more. This section goes into detail about the key platforms and how to develop a social media strategy.

Planning social

What is your goal?

Before joining social media think about why you want to use it. Your goal might be to make more industry contacts, engage with your audiences, get more consulting gigs or build brand awareness.

Having a goal will give you some direction when determining your social media activities as well as measuring your overall success.

As an expert, your aims may include:

- Positioning yourself as an expert on niche subject matter.
- Developing your reputation as a thought leader.
- Building a community around your personal brand.
- Raising awareness about your profile with your target audience.
- Getting feedback about and gauging people's interest in your subject matter.
- Connecting with influencers who may help raise your profile.

Have a think about specific goals and objectives for what you want to achieve. These will also help to measure your success and plan more effective ongoing strategies. Examples of your objectives may include:

- Build your Twitter followers to 500 and retweet or engage at least once per day.
- Get 300 page 'likes' on your Facebook page and get one comment per day.
- Develop relationships with influencers of LinkedIn and Twitter by contributing to their conversations.

Choose a platform

When starting with social media it may be a good idea to focus on one or two social media platforms first. Then, once you've mastered one or two platforms you can move on to another. Taking on too many at once can be very overwhelming and may be less effective.

When choosing the right platforms for you, think about which will help you achieve your goal. You also need to consider the best platforms to help you reach your target audiences. (These will be the platforms your target audiences are most active on.)

Define your area of expertise

You know your area of expertise, so make sure you position yourself as an expert by showcasing your expert knowledge in a particular area.

Make sure your profile reflects this niche by discussing it in your bio and posting and commenting on expert articles about this area. Don't deviate from your area of expertise as it will dilute your personal brand.

Get your information ready

Before creating a profile on a social media platform make sure you have all your information ready.

Write a short bio, create a cover image and logo/avatar image in the correct sizes and have your company information, such as contact details, ready. Having a complete profile will help people find you, immediately understand what you do and relate to you.

What content will you post?

You need to think about the type of content you will post on social media. Before you sign up to social media it's a good idea to prepare content to ensure you have something to post.

To help you plan your content, also consider developing a content calendar. This will help you make the most of the content you have.

Some ideas for content may include posting a link to your blog, posting a link to an expert article, current industry news, photos, videos, questions, infographics and media coverage.

Build followers

Once you have created a profile on social media you need to start building your followers. One way to do this is by informing your friends, clients and networks about your profile and encouraging them to follow or connect with you. Include the URL to your social media profile in all of your marketing materials, business cards, email signatures, newsletters, website and more.

Another way to build followers is by posting relevant content on your profile, commenting on other people's profiles and engaging your customers.

Measure success

Think about how you will measure your social media involvement to determine its success. This can also help you to discover whether your activities are working and what you can do to improve your results.

To measure success, you will need to monitor your social media channels. You can use a paid or free social media monitoring service, or develop your own system. The easiest way to monitor your platforms is usually through the free data and analytics tools provided by the platforms i.e. LinkedIn Analytics for Company Pages, Facebook Insights and Twitter Analytics.

Managing your time on social media

We've all experienced it - the social media time warp - where we log onto Facebook or other social media platforms and don't resurface until hours later.

However, just because social media can be time-consuming, it doesn't mean you shouldn't do it.

You just need to learn some time-saving tricks to make the most of your time on social media and use it more effectively.

Here are some of my top tips to help you manage your time.

Use scheduling tools

Scheduling tools such as TweetDeck and Hootsuite allow you to schedule your posts in advance. For example TweetDeck allows you to create your tweets and chose different times to automatically post them during the day. This means you could spend half an hour on Monday morning setting up all your posts for the rest of the week.

Facebook also allows you to schedule posts straight from your profile page. Even though you've scheduled your posts you should still log into your social media platforms to respond to comments.

Have a strategy

If you use social media without a purpose or a strategy you will waste a lot of time. This usually occurs when you spend hours looking through your social media accounts and are unsure what to post or comment on. You need a social media strategy to help you define your goals and objectives for using social media and to make the most of your time spent on each platform.

Your strategy will help you define what to post, when to post it, who will be in charge of posting, how to reply to comments and how to measure your engagement.

Choose a platform

You may find social media difficult to handle if you are juggling every social media platform available. The best idea is to focus on one social media platform and become a confident user before moving on to another.

Choose a social media platform your target audiences use and start engaging with them. Once you have a community of loyal followers they may be more willing to connect with you on other platforms as well.

Cross linking

Use your time effectively by posting the same material on multiple social media sites. For example the content you post on LinkedIn can also be tweeted, Facebooked or Pinned.

Tools, such as Tweetdeck and Hootsuite, allow you to share your content automatically across all your social media platforms. However, you need to make sure you tailor each post so it will be suitable for each social media platform.

Use Bit.ly

Bit.ly is a free URL shortening service which allows you to easily save and share your favourite links from around the web. After pasting a URL into bit.ly you are given the option to share the link with others via Facebook, Twitter or your email account, copy the link, add notes to the bit.ly link or add the bit.ly link into a bundle. Bundles can be used to organise and share all your links into one page making it easy to save your bit.ly links and find them later.

In addition to its URL shortening services, you are able to track the statistics for any bit.ly link you create. From these statistics you can find out insights about your bit.ly links, such as seeing which social networks are driving the most traffic to your link.

What social media platforms are right for you?

With so many social media platforms available, it can be hard to figure out which one will deliver the best results. However, there are a few things to consider before choosing a social media platform.

Remember that the platform you use has to be aligned not only with your aims, but also with your capabilities. Social media can be quite time-consuming, so if you're a busy person you need to make sure you can build it into your day.

An option may be to start off with one social media platform, systematise the way you use it and if you feel you have time, set up a second one.

To begin using social media it will be best to examine the characteristics of each platform and determine which one best suits your goals, business values and target audiences.

To help you choose the platforms that work for you, here are five of the top social media sites and how they can help your business:

Facebook

Is a great site to use for customer engagement, feedback and brand development for your products and services. However, it may not the best social media platform to drive traffic to your webpage.

Twitter

Twitter can be used quite successfully to drive organic traffic to your website as the more followers you have the more people will see your tweets and click on your links. The challenge, however, is creating an interesting and quality tweet in only 140 characters.

YouTube

If you have a funny cat video than you'll get heaps of hits on your YouTube channel, but if not, it can be hard to build an audience. It is fantastic way to get opinions and information about your business into the public in a visual and creative way. If you plan on presenting and speaking, YouTube is essential to showcase your presentation style.

LinkedIn

If you want to position yourself and your brand as an expert in a specific industry, this is the site for you! LinkedIn is a professional site that allows you to build connections with people who will assist you to build your personal brand. Take the time to research and join groups that are relevant to you and your potential audience.

Facebook

There are over one billion active Facebook users worldwide and about 60 percent of them log in every day. The average user is connected to 80 community pages, groups and events – all opportunities for brand promotion.

So it makes sense that a Facebook page is a great tool for building your profile and engaging with people that will help you achieve this.

Most people have a personal Facebook page. You can use your own personal Facebook page to share information about your area of expertise and/or you can set up a Facebook business page.

When deciding between these two strategies consider whether you are comfortable turning your personal Facebook page into a business tool. I would suggest that you create a Facebook business/product page and keep your personal page for personal use.

Note: If you haven't created a Facebook page before, you can look up Facebook's 'about pages' section for instructions on how to build your page, including great examples.

Look and feel

The look and feel of your page is important. It should be a place that attracts visitors and makes them want to return. Below are various features which you can customise to make the most of your page.

About section

The about section of your Facebook page is the place to include a brief description and your URL to your website or blog.

Cover photo

As we all know, visuals capture people's attention much more than words. So the first thing you can do to customise your Facebook page is upload a cover image (851 x 315 pixels). Choose an image that is representative of your brand and don't be afraid to get creative with it. Think about changing it every couple of weeks so the update goes into your feed. Don't forget you can add a link or an offer on the cover photo such as an eBook offer or upcoming course.

Organise your views and tabs

Your tabs are located below the cover photo on the right-hand side and you can have up to 20 of them. Only the first four tabs will be visible to fans – the rest can be accessed by clicking on the drop down arrow, which few people do – so make sure these are your four most important tabs and that they align to your brand and your objectives.

As an expert, you might find the following tabs useful:

- **Photos** are one of the most engaging types of media (apart from video) and are a good way to document your expertise, media exposure and speaking opportunities. Note this is the only tab you can't change as one of the four visible tabs.
- **Events** you speak at or are involved in and charity events you support can be added on your Facebook page.
- A **blog** tab or a link to your blog is a great way to cross-promote your other activities.
- A **contact** tab will provide that 'call to action' fans and potential readers need to connect with you directly.

Create content

Great content is essential for every social media platform, and Facebook is a platform where people expect to be entertained more than simply informed. When someone 'likes' your page they are opting in to receive company news, marketing messages and information about products, so give them what they want.

Here are some ideas to help you create Facebook posts:

- **Photos** – Share behind the scenes photos, videos and updates. Not only do they get more clicks and likes on your page, photos are a powerful way of establishing an emotional connection with your followers. Ask someone to take photos of you when speaking, or short videos of you doing workshops. When adding a link to an expert article, also upload an image.

- **Like baiting** - Create posts that encourage fans to 'like' them. Make a statement that people may feel passionate about and ask them to 'like' if they agree.
- **Asking questions** - Ask your fans questions they will want to answer. When thinking about questions make them relatable to a wide audience – the more people can connect with the question on a personal level, the more likely they are to participate.
- **Share viral posts** - See what's trending online that relates to your industry and niche and post updates or comments.
- Share **newsworthy articles** and news stories relevant to your expertise.
- Link to **blog posts** - Cross promote your blog by sharing every new post on your Facebook page.
- Offer **tips** related to your expertise.

HOT TIP: a standard text update for a company page won't appear in the timeline as much as an update with a photo and a link. So aim to use links and photos to give more views.

Content calendar

Planning your content is the easiest way to make the most of your Facebook page. Develop a simple posting strategy or a content calendar similar to the one below that shows which types of posts you intend to publish each day. This will also help you stay on track and have an overview of when you need to post.

For example, CP Communications page content strategy includes:

Post three times a day and posts can include:

- CP Communications articles, PR Sydney blog articles or Social Media Sydney blog articles
- Interesting external articles
- Client coverage

- CP Communications coverage
- Photos and commentary from events
- PR and social media tips of the week
- Gorgeous Tuesdays pictures (Cute pictures of animals)
- What's on Wednesday (Information on upcoming events)

Day to be posted on	Date	Time	Topic of post	Type of post	Post content	Link
Monday	20/10	9.30am	Inter-esting article	Link	"How do you develop great Facebook content? Find our top tips here"	Link to article
Monday	20/10	1:30pm	Blog post	Image & Link	5 ways to get amazing me-dia coverage.	Link to PR Sydney blog
Monday	20/10	3:00pm	Image	Image	We hope you had a relaxing weekend. How did you spend your weekend?	No link

How often you post content depends on how interesting and valuable your content is, but as a general rule, update your page around three times a day.

The best way to learn what works for your Facebook page is to practice and experiment. Only experience can truly teach you what your target audience wants and how to encourage them to engage.

Schedule it

You can schedule posts on Facebook straight from the business' Facebook page. After typing in the status update you will see a clock symbol in the bottom left-hand corner. By clicking on this symbol you can choose the year, month, date and time you want the post to appear.

Scheduling your posts is a great way to save time on Facebook because it allows you to set up your posts for any length of time. It's also a helpful tool to allow you to schedule posts over the weekend and continue posting while you may not be at work.

Boosting posts

If you want to increase the reach of your Facebook posts you can use the promoted posts feature. With this feature you can pay to help your post be seen by more people.

Boosting a post means your posts are shown to more people in the desktop and mobile News Feeds which will encourage likes, comments and shares. When people engage with your post, their friends may see it as a story in their own News Feed. This means you'll reach more people. This is a great way to communicate important information to a larger target audience and amplify the reach for certain posts.

You can also promote your business page to get more Page likes from specific target audiences. If you are just starting out and building your page likes, it's worth considering investing in this type of advertising.

Build an audience

At the top of your Facebook business page, you will see the button 'Build Audience'. This function will give you the option of inviting your existing contacts from a variety of platforms. You can invite your personal Facebook friends to 'like' the page. Facebook also suggest friends to invite to your page.

Build your number of fans by spreading the word through your marketing channels, like your website, email signature and enewsletters. Facebook advertising is also good value and an effective way of building awareness of your page.

Social media is about having two-way discussions and engaging in conversations, which acts as another online promotional technique. So join Facebook groups, like pages which are all relevant to your expertise and start commenting on their posts and sharing useful or entertaining content (never in a promotional way).

Monitor your page

Facebook Insights, which can be found on the top of your Facebook page "See Insights", allows you to monitor and measure your page's performance (e.g. likes, weekly reach, performance of each status update, etc.) and export this data to keep a record of your progress on a monthly, fortnightly or weekly basis.

If you are unsure about what you want to measure, you can use the data displayed by Facebook Insights to come up with realistic, yet challenging, targets.

For example, you may like to increase the number of total likes from 50 people to 65 people in six weeks. Or increase page views from an average of 39 weekly views to an average of 50 views per week in two months.

Take a look and see which posts are getting the most engagement, and which aren't working and tailor your strategy accordingly.

Set Facebook Targets

Take some time to think about what you want to achieve from Facebook and set your targets.
Open your Action Step and start now.

Visit **www.UnknownToExpertBonus.com**
For Your FREE Bonus Action Step Content

ACTION
STEP

LinkedIn

LinkedIn is a social media platform that has been specifically created for professionals. It's a powerful business tool and provides a great way to stay in touch with connections, create relationships with new people, and identify and connect with potential clients.

LinkedIn can also help you increase your visibility and position yourself as a leader in your industry. One way of doing so is by ensuring that regular updates related to your field of expertise are made on your profile. You should also find groups in your industry and your clients' industries and join relevant and engaging discussions.

Unlike Facebook and Twitter where you can mix personal with professional, LinkedIn is specifically for business and professionals.

Personal profile

The first place to start is to update your profile. Unlike Facebook, LinkedIn is fully searchable – both from within LinkedIn and on the open web. Your personal profile is similar to a resume (but so much more) and serves as a summary of your work history.

Your LinkedIn profile needs to be well-organised, thought out, well-written and most importantly – showcase your expertise. A fully completed LinkedIn profile shows up in 40 percent more searches, so ensure you fill in as much as possible.

Photo

Be aware, your photo says a lot about you (including not having a photo). Unless you are in an industry where casual or cool is ok, avoid this look at all costs.

Some things to steer clear of: sunglasses on head or on face, wedding photos and personal hobby shots – keep these shots for your Facebook. Ensure your photo is professional looking, in focus, has good lighting and a plain background and truly just a head and shoulder shot. You want to look good enough for people to click into your profile.

Title

To take full advantage of the search capability, add keyword phrases to your heading and title you believe are most commonly being used to search for someone like you. As an example, I am CEO of CP Communications but my title on LinkedIn is Public Relations and Social Media specialist, making it much easier for people looking for PR or social media services to find me.

Also ensure you add your most up-to-date contact details so people can easily contact you. I use LinkedIn to find suppliers and people to do business with all the time and a pet hate of mine is when they haven't added their contact details!

Customised URL

In this section you can customise your LinkedIn URL. Instead of having a URL that is a whole lot of random numbers and letters, you want it to be your name. This is really easy to do.

Go to Profile and click Edit, then Edit Contact Info. At the bottom of the Contact Info box you'll see your URL. Select Edit. In the bottom, right-hand corner you'll see a box labelled Your Public Profile URL. Click on Customise your Public Profile URL. Change this to be just your name with no spaces.

Summary

Your summary is critical. It needs to outline your expertise as well as highlight what type of work you do. Use a professional, friendly tone and write in 1st person. Add information about your experience/expertise, current role, briefly previous roles and interests/specialities. It needs to be under 2000 characters and don't forget you can add media i.e. photo, videos to this section.

Here is my summary as an example:

Are you looking to grow your sales pipeline and stand out from competitors?

If you're a business owner, CEO, Managing Director or Marketing Manager, consider this: The right combination of media exposure and social dialogue can be the spark needed to amplify your reputation and boost sales. Using these strategies you have an opportunity to be seen as an industry leader, giving you a distinct competitive advantage.

I am the founder and Managing Director of CP Communications, an acclaimed PR and social media agency known for producing amazing results. We were one of the first PR agencies in Australia to offer social media services and we continue to lead the industry in combining social strategies with PR.

Our clients love us because we do whatever it takes to get the results they deserve.

I am listed as one of the top 100 PR people to follow on Twitter, and recognised as one of Australia's top 25 business bloggers. I am a media commentator and my views on social media and PR have been extensively published in media such as SMH, CEO Magazine, The Australian, Sky Business News, B&T, BRW, Women's Agenda, SmartCompany and LeadingCompany.

I am also an in-demand speaker on the topics of PR and social media and have presented for numerous conferences and business forums including Problogger, Digital Marketing Forum, Women on Boards, CEO Institute, CBA Women in Focus, City of Sydney, University of Technology, Macquarie University and many more.

CP Communications develops comprehensive, creative and results driven public relations and social media programs including:

• Strategic public relations
• Social media strategy & management
• Media releases, editorial and article development
• PR and social media training.

Follow me on Twitter @CatrionaPollard

E: cp@cpcommunications.com.au

W: http://www.cpcommunications.com.au

B: http://www.PublicRelationsSydney.com.au

T: @CPCPR

F: http://www.facebook.com/CPCommunications

Y: http://www.youtube.com/publicrelationstips

Publications

A little used section is called 'Publications', which is perfect for experts and thought leaders as you can upload links to your online media coverage or any publications, eBooks or articles you have written.

You can also add projects, languages, organisations, honours and awards, test scores, courses, patents, certifications, volunteering and causes.

28

ACTION STEP

Write Your LinkedIn Profile

It's essential you have an up-to-date professional personal LinkedIn profile, so take action, jump to the Action Step and follow the steps to write your profile.

Visit **www.UnknownToExpertBonus.com**
For Your FREE Bonus Action Step Content

Recommendations

Recommendations are an effective way of promoting yourself and your business. People who are happy with your work can write a brief testimonial and post it on your LinkedIn profile.

You can ask your clients or co-workers to post recommendations, which future employers and clients can view to gauge your skills and level of trustworthiness. Obviously, what goes around comes around, so you should also take the time to write recommendations for other people you've had good experiences with.

I suggest you send an email asking for a recommendation, rather than through LinkedIn as it is more personal.

Connections

There are a number of simple ways to build your network and connect with people through LinkedIn.

Import your contacts

You can import your business email contacts from Outlook, Gmail, and Yahoo into LinkedIn to help broaden your network.

To do this:

- In LinkedIn click the Add Connections link.
- Select the relevant email service. You will be asked to login to the email service.
- A list of people from your contact list will appear.
- Select/deselect who you would like to add. Select add connections.

LinkedIn suggestions

LinkedIn will also help you make connections by suggesting who it thinks you should connect with.

LinkedIn 'People you may know' is located on the right-hand side of your profile and allows you to quickly scan users and send invitations to them to link with you.

Inform people

Let people know you're on LinkedIn so they can link with you through the platform. Do this by including a link to your profile on your email signature, putting it on your business card, posting it on other social media sites and telling people you meet to encourage them to connect with you.

When connecting with people be personal and let them know how you are connected. Don't use the auto connection template.

 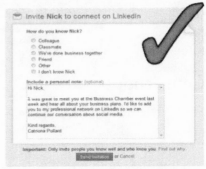

Draft a LinkedIn Invitation to Connect

Start connecting with people who can assist in you moving from unknown to expert. Jump to the Action Step and draft a LinkedIn invitation to connect message.

ACTION STEP

Visit **www.UnknownToExpertBonus.com**
For Your FREE Bonus Action Step Content

Sharing content

This is one of the most critical elements on LinkedIn for experts and thought leaders. Associating your personal brand with the content of your posts and discussions makes you stand out and become synonymous with that content. This builds credibility and trust.

Every time you update your status on LinkedIn it will go into the news feed of your LinkedIn connections.

Make it a habit to post updates regularly (ideally you should do this at least once a day).

You also have an ability to 'like', 'comment' or 'share' your connections' updates. If there is someone you would particularly like to build a relationship with, you could initiate a conversation by interacting with their status updates.

Type of content to share

Post an interesting article, blog post or quote relating to your area of expertise or industry. Here are some content suggestions.

- Any article or video from a respected publication e.g. *Sydney Morning Herald*, *Forbes*, *BRW*, etc.
- Your media coverage (online).
- Infographics.
- Whitepapers.
- Industry surveys.
- Thought-leading articles from your industry.

To save time, you can copy relevant updates from Facebook and Twitter onto LinkedIn that are of a professional tone.

When sharing a URL, simply paste the URL into the status box and the article link and image will automatically appear.

The trick is not to simply share the URL, but to add an editorial comment that relates to your area of expertise.

Here are some examples I have used:

A media pitch is a waste of time if it isn't relevant to the journalist you're sending it to. Getting this right requires researching your target media and understanding what topics they cover, who their audience is as well as their deadlines. Sending your pitch to the most relevant journalist at a publication is critical. There's no use sending a technology story to an education writer. (http://publicrelationssydney.com.au/index.php/tips-for-creating-an-excellent-media-list/)

LinkedIn is the perfect vehicle for business professionals to build thought leadership. Even just updating your profile status on a regular basis can highlight your expertise. However, don't just post a link, share an insight or an opinion that others might find interesting. (http://socialmediasydney.net.au/how-to-use-linkedin-to-build-your-thought-leadership/)

HOT TIP: Media contacts

Journalists use LinkedIn too, just like other professionals. If you have done a media interview, or interacted with a journalist in some way, connect with them on LinkedIn.

Next time they are writing an article about something within your areas of expertise, they may remember you and ring you for some quotes for an article.

Don't barrage them by trying to communicate with them every day, but an occasional comment on something they have posted will go a long way in ensuring you are remembered by them.

The key to LinkedIn (and all social media) is to treat it like you would real life networking. Don't just talk about yourself but add value to your connections, and you will start to reap the rewards.

Write and Share Content on LinkedIn

Write and share content on LinkedIn. I guarantee doing this regularly on your area of expertise will significantly increase your profile. Open your Action Step and start now.

ACTION STEP

Visit **www.UnknownToExpertBonus.com**
For Your FREE Bonus Action Step Content

LinkedIn groups

There are thousands of groups already created on LinkedIn. Even if you have your own one, you should join others relating your industry, and the industries of your clients or customers, and become an active member.

LinkedIn groups are a great place to share your expertise and knowledge with people outside your contacts through either posting your own articles or blog posts, or commenting on others' updates.

Don't just share your own links though; ensure you are adding value to the conversation by commenting on other posts and answering questions if you know the answers.

Start your own group

You may be a member of many LinkedIn groups, but have you ever thought about starting a LinkedIn group? It's an effective way of showcasing your expertise and building your profile as a thought leader in your industry.

Think strategically about what your target audiences are going to be searching for when looking for groups to join.

When you start a group, invite all of your contacts to join, and ask your team members to do the same. This is a great way to build up membership quickly.

Groups are not 'set and forget'. You need to start interesting discussions by posting articles or blog posts to highlight your knowledge and further build your profile as an expert in your industry.

Starting a LinkedIn group is a great way to be exposed to people in your industry or profession and raise your profile as an expert. If you're willing to make the commitment, follow these tips to best manage and build a LinkedIn group:

- Depending on your privacy settings, you may need to approve comments before they appear on the wall. If this is the case, check the page once or twice daily to keep the conversation flowing.
- Until members begin initiating discussions, you should post twice a week. A good tactic is one post that asks a question, and one that links to an interesting article that is relevant to the topic of the group.
- If there are already active discussions, contribute to these rather than starting another discussion.

Your LinkedIn group might take a few weeks to begin attracting members and generating discussion. But by following these tips you should find that before long you'll be in charge of a lively discussion – a great way to position yourself as the expert in your field!

Twitter

Twitter can be a great avenue to demonstrate your expertise and gain a following of people interested in hearing what you have to say.

With Twitter you can establish two-way real-time communication with potential advocates, industry affiliates and professionals from external fields and industries whose ideas and advice, in the form of tweets, could lend to your success.

To build your followers naturally, share links to helpful or insightful articles related to your expertise (this includes your own articles and blogs, but also those from other sources), cross-promote your LinkedIn discussions, follow people in your industry and target audiences and interact with them.

Once you have good Twitter relationships you then have the means to potentially communicate to a much larger audience than you would normally have access to.

Tweeting tips

Find your niche

Make a list of all your keywords and topics and find people and organisations to follow who are interested in these topics. By tweeting on a particular issue, you are positioning yourself as a thought leader in that field and building upon your credibility among the online community. Just as one would be quoted in a newspaper or magazine, the more people who trust what you say and believe in your expertise, the more likely you are to be retweeted.

Choose your timing wisely

Depending on the nature of your followers, certain times of the day and week will have higher Twitter traffic than others. Statistics show that the best time to tweet is mid-afternoon early in the week. Linking back to the previous point, it is important to gain an understanding of the Twitter habits of your followers. Consider whether they can tweet during work hours, or whether the majority of them are overseas in different time zones. Then you can schedule your tweets to match their routines.

Engage with your community

Being an active participant in online conversations will not only help build your online profile, but will strengthen the relationships between you and your online community. Retweet generously, respond to mentions where relevant, thank your followers when they retweet you, and when you're in need of some instant exposure, ask your followers to retweet you – if you've treated them well in the past, they're more than likely to return the favour.

Create lists

A great way to connect and keep up with influencers on Twitter is to make lists. They will give you a way to meaningfully organise your Twitter feed and to monitor what's happening with the people and businesses you are interested in.

What to tweet

Before you start sending tweets out to your community of Twitter followers, ask yourself why they are following you. Do they know you personally? Are they looking for advice? What are your target audiences interested in? Do they read your blog, or are they a fan of your Facebook page? Once you understand what they are looking for, shape your Twitter content to meet their expectations and demonstrate that you are dedicated to building a relationship and providing value.

Like with Facebook, the best Twitter strategy is to create a content calendar that has a mixture of expert-related, personal and interesting posts including:

Personal tweets

Tweet about your views on current affairs, daily activities, upcoming events – the world is your oyster!

Newsworthy issues

As an expert, people expect you to be knowledgeable in your field and to keep up to date with industry trends. Make sure you validate this expectation by sharing newsworthy articles and new trends that concern your subject matter.

Interesting articles or blogs

Twitter's value comes largely from sharing information that others will find useful or interesting. People who share engaging content tend to accumulate followers rapidly because people quickly realise the value of following a person who has so much to give. So try to become such a person by regularly sharing something that people want to read. Find popular blogs or websites related to your industry and post links.

Highlights from your life or business

People value emotional connections so make it easy for them to form such a connection with you by sending out tweets that communicate your personal journey.

Retweets

If someone you are following says something in their tweet that you agree with or like, you can promote their tweet to all your followers by retweeting it. This means that the tweet will be seen by the tweeter's followers, your followers and the followers of anyone else who retweets it. This is a great way of connecting to new people and building two-way communication.

Participating in discussions

Find out what topics are trending and conversations happening on Twitter by using the 'Discover' tab and the search function. Contribute to or initiate conversations that relate to your expertise.

Make sure you use hashtags so that your tweets become part of the conversation. For example, if you tweet about marketing strategies for SMEs, end your tweet with #marketing. This means your tweet will be sorted into a category with all other tweets containing the #marketing hashtag. This allows other people who have used it to see your tweet, which means you are more likely to attract the followers you want.

Decide on how often you are going to tweet. I aim to tweet around four times daily my personal account @CatrionaPollard and on the CP Communications Twitter account, @CPCPR.

Monitoring Twitter

Like with all social media, in order to get the best results you should monitor and measure how your Twitter handle is performing.

There are different Twitter tools that allow you to measure different criteria and see where you stand in comparison to other Twitter users and brands.

Some examples of free monitoring tools include:

- Crowdbooster which gives you an overview of follower growth, number of mentions and retweets your account receives, and the number of influential followers you have.
- Topsy is a similar tool which also allows you to see all of your tweets and sort them according to type (photo, link, video).
- Klout is an influence measuring tool which can be used to measure your influence and activity on Twitter as well as on other social media.

Using these tools will give you a better idea of how effective your Twitter efforts are and how engaged you are with your community.

Get Tweeting!

Develop your own tweets.
Jump over to your Action Step to start now.

Visit **www.UnknownToExpertBonus.com**
For Your FREE Bonus Action Step Content

YouTube

YouTube allows you to reach an audience of millions, all around the world. It allows you to be the director of your own videos and to dictate exactly what happens and what you talk about, in contrast to television interviews.

YouTube can serve as a visual and absolutely free medium for sharing your expertise and building your profile. There are additional benefits to using YouTube including the fact that, as the platform is owned by Google, it is highly ranked by the search engine.

Visual content has high rates of engagement amongst audiences and is SEO (search engine optimisation) friendly. In addition, it can be syndicated across multiple sites, which means it can be embedded in your blog or included in an enewsletter.

It also has an important branding benefit: it allows viewers to make a personal connection with you as an individual.

The first thing you will need to do is start your own channel on YouTube. This will allow you to create a collection of videos, edit them and refer to them on an ongoing basis.

When you have set up your channel you can begin creating your videos.

Different video formats

Online tutorials

YouTube has become a thriving environment where people from all over the world share their knowledge with others. As an expert in your field you will be able to share valuable learnings with your audience.

You've probably come across video tutorials explaining how you can learn to dance samba, use Photoshop, learn a language, write a better resume and much, much more. There is no reason why you can't do the same to build your brand.

Simply identify what you would like to teach your viewers (that relates to your expertise). Write out a script, which includes an introduction with the purpose of your tutorial (what you will be teaching), the body, including the key points, as well as the conclusion, including what you hope the viewers will take away.

HOT TIP: Use an autocue app so you don't need to remember what to say! This has helped me enormously. I use Teleprompt+ for iPad.

Interview with the expert (you!)

You don't have to be an experienced video producer to create a simple video interview. All you need is the help of another person to read out pre-prepared questions and reply with answers you have thought through.

Draw up a list of questions that give the viewer an insight into you and your background.

Practice doing the interview with a timer to make sure that your interview doesn't exceed three minutes – videos tend to do better when they are more succinct.

The beauty of pre-recording is that you have complete control over what goes up online. Do as many takes as you need to get your message right.

Interview with another expert

What better way of positioning yourself as an expert than by interviewing someone who is a guru in your industry, or best-selling author, or a highly regarded thought leader in your field. Often, they are happy to be interviewed, particularly if they have something to promote such as a new book or seminar series. You need to pitch them (or their publicist) the idea, proving the value for them, but if you don't ask you won't receive!

Creating engaging content

Now that you are familiar with different video formats, you can delve deeper into what makes a successful video.

A successful video is not necessarily a viral video (these can be difficult to create and to control if they go wrong). Rather, a successful video communicates the creator's purpose clearly and in an engaging manner; it is aligned with the creator's brand and is able to influence the viewer in a way that the creator of the video wants.

Length

The shorter you can make your videos the better. People have an increasingly short attention span due to the amount of information now available to them. For your tutorial videos you can be a bit more flexible with time but try to limit the duration of the video to three minutes maximum. Try a series of 30 second tips.

Structure

Have a clear structure in mind before creating each video. This might mean writing out a short script or outline to help you get organised. Have intro and closing segments (outros) to boost your brand. If you have a high quality logo or background image you would use for your business, use these as part of your intro and closing.

The actual content you include in these depends on what you think is most crucial for your audience. Always include your name and contact details so viewers can get in touch or find out more about you.

How to make sure your video is found

- **Add an SEO-friendly description** - Add key information in the description below the video once you have uploaded it to YouTube.
- **Add tags** - The reason for adding tags is simple - it helps people find your video when they search. Make a list of all the keywords which are relevant to the video topic, you, your industry and your expertise.
- **Add categories** - Adding the category to your video has the same purpose as the tags - to make your video easier to locate once you're on the YouTube website.
- **Promote** - Spread the message about your video by letting your

networks know about it. Put it up on your website, tweet about it, post an update on Facebook and LinkedIn and include it in your email newsletter. Just make sure that as many people as possible know about your new video. After all, it's there to be shared.

Plan Your YouTube Video

Now it's time to take action and plan your next YouTube video. Take a look at the Action Step and start the planning, content creation and filming!

Visit **www.UnknownToExpertBonus.com**
For Your FREE Bonus Action Step Content

Google+

Google+ is Google's answer to a social media platform and it has real potential if you have the time to engage. It is certainly an excellent way to improve your SEO.

Use Google+ circles effectively

Google+ circles allow you to group or categorise your contacts so you can tailor your content to a particular audience. For a personal Google+ page this may mean dividing your contacts into friends, family and co-workers.

For a business page this allows you to segment your market and target each group differently. You may choose to divide contacts into groups according to theme or interest area and engage with them on that level.

You can also find relevant people, pages and posts to add to your circles, by doing a keyword or hashtag search, extending your network even further.

Share content which engages your audiences

The best way to engage your target audiences is to share content that is relevant to them. By dividing your contacts into circles by interest, you immediately know which content will work for which circle. Sharing visual content such as images or video is also a good way to drive engagement.

It's important to remember when sharing content your goal is to drive engagement. Google+ is a two-way channel. Ask questions, join conversations and start debate.

Maximise SEO opportunities

Google+ is an excellent way to improve SEO. Google uses data gleaned from Google+ to help determine how data is ranked and personalise a search experience. This can mean better SEO for your business. By sharing your content in Google+ you can also drive traffic back to your website.

You should also promote your Google+ page on your website to help your customers find you. Add a Google+ badge to give people an easy way to navigate straight to your Google+ business page.

Join Communities and Hangouts

Google+ Communities and Hangouts are groups that bring together like-minded users to discuss issues of interest. They can be a great way to engage users with your brand.

Communities allow users to post on a topic of interest. There are over 50,000 communities on Google+. Hangouts are live chats or interactions which engage users in real time. Brands can host chats, competitions, or seek feedback through using Hangouts.

Getting the most out of Google+ mostly relies on jumping in and getting involved. See what other people are doing and pick up useful ways to engage with your audience.

Instagram

Instagram is one of the key social media platforms. Although many people use it for private purposes, it also has applications for businesses.

Although Instagram has been around a while, it's the new kid on the block in terms of social media for business purposes.

Instagram is an app which allows users to share photos and short videos with their friends and followers. It can be accessed with an iPhone as well as Android and Blackberry.

The way Instagram works, is that you take a photo or shoot a short video, apply one of around 12 different filters over it, tag the location and add a description. Users can tag their followers and add hashtags. Instagram includes functionality that allows photos to be automatically uploaded to Facebook, Twitter, Flickr and email. Photos appear in a linear timeline.

The language of Instagram

Like every social channel, Instagram has its own language. Hashtags are really important – if I take a photo of a sunset from our offices (which I do often!) I'll attach a hashtag #sunset so people looking for sunset shots can find it.

The use of hashtags means you are able to select which search category your pictures appear in. This allows you to reach a wide audience by targeting certain searches, much like keyword research for SEO. The greatest feature of Instagram is the ability to interact with users beyond words.

Strategies

Take a look at some of the most popular brands/companies and how they utilise Instagram. For example, the eBay Instagram account is filled with interesting photos accompanied by relevant tags and captions. eBay has cleverly marketed their website by being subtle and offering something of value to users.

The first thing you should do is link your Instagram with your other social media accounts. Since Instagram photos can't directly link to a page, you have to direct people via your captions. Your profile page should include your actual URL or links to other social networks where they can find out more about your services and what you can offer. Instagram can be compared to a storefront; it is a sort of visual merchandising for your company.

To get started and noticed on Instagram you should start following and participating in small groups within Instagram. Once you are a regular and active follower, people will start to take notice of your comments and photos and you will begin to see a rise in interactions relating to your photos.

Be selective about what you put on Instagram; always put your best pictures first. Make sure the photos are of the highest quality you can manage. Try to take photos which reveal a bit of character and personality to your business, this will show that you are a living and breathing human just like your followers.

If you continue to release regular updates on Instagram you will soon see the same results you are experiencing on Facebook and Twitter. It takes more time to prepare nice photos and to go out and actually take them, but in the end it is worth it to capitalise on an opportunity that isn't offered anywhere else on the internet.

Pinterest

Have you heard the saying "a picture paints a thousand words"? Well your business can do just that on social media platform Pinterest.

Pinterest is a social media site where you can create online bulletin boards and 'pin' your favourite images and videos to it.

You can create a variety of bulletin boards in any category imaginable. Your followers can then view your images, like them, add a comment and repin them to their own boards. Each image includes a link to its original website, which makes sharing images and websites easy.

The benefit of Pinterest over the more text-heavy Twitter and Facebook is that images on Pinterest can convey their messages to the audience with just a quick glance.

It isn't a broadcast mechanism and doesn't encourage product pushing, so you need to be creative and take a different approach to Twitter and Facebook.

Pinterest boards

The key to Pinterest is creating boards that convey your business story. For example, at CP Communications we have boards that reflect the work the business does and who we are.

For instance, we have a board that showcases the charities we support and a board that has images that use the colours of CP Communications' logo (red and purple). We also have a 'gorgeous' board, which features cute animal pictures, a sunset board that has pictures of sunsets taken from the office, as well as 'CP in the media' and 'behind the scenes' boards. Our most popular board is 'tips for PR and social media'.

If you are a catering expert you might have a board that features produce that you use, or a board that relates to canapés, or one that features slow cooking or organic food.

If you have a wedding business you will have boards that feature pictures of yummy cakes, beautiful dresses and favourite honeymoon destinations.

It's all about the language

If you're going to use Pinterest for your business, hashtags are essential. Whenever CP Communications pins to its PR and social media boards, we will use #PR or #socialmedia so anyone searching for pins on that topic can find our material.

There are also a number of sharing options. Each image can be shared on Facebook and Twitter, embedded on blogs and external sites (which is great for link building) and the URL can be shared via email.

It's also really important to have visually interesting photos because the more interesting they are, the more they will be repinned.

Tracking and strategy

It's essential to have a strategy and understand what you will get out of being on Pinterest, who you are targeting and what they want to see.

Use the Pinreach tracking tool to help you measure your followers, which pins attract the most interest (so you can focus on building up these types of pins in the future) and change your strategy according to the feedback and data you receive.

Pinterest shouldn't be used purely for advertising purposes because your followers may view your content as spam and disconnect from you. Your business should become actively involved in the Pinterest community by posting useful content and repinning or commenting on other users' images.

HOT TIPS: Pinterest

- **Engage with your target audience:** You can share a behind the scenes look into your business by pinning images of you presenting or office activities. This will help create personal relationships and connections with your clients.
- **Learn from your customers:** Brands can learn from their followers as they are offering a lot of information about their personal interests.

- **Run competitions**: You can ask Pinterest users to pin images to your board to receive benefits or prizes as part of a competition or special offer. This will help to raise awareness of your business and gain new customers.
- **Crowdsourcing**: Ask people to pin pictures of themselves with your product and repin them on a themed board.
- **Reach target customers**: You can reach your target customers by creating boards in categories appropriate to your target customers. Currently, the majority of users on Pinterest are female, which will benefit businesses whose target customers are women.
- **Drive traffic to your website**: You can pin images with a link back to your website to help increase your website traffic.
- **Promote your products**: You can post images of your business' products and services with a link to your website where they can purchase them. This can help to increase your sales and customers.
- **Promote your success**: Post images of media coverage, success stories or client case studies to promote your business' achievements.

The beginning

So now you have moved from unknown to recognised expert. You are truly a known expert.

Congratulations. You are a bright shining star.

How does it feel? A huge whoop whoop, fist pump and happy dance – all rolled into one.

However, it's not the end, it's the beginning.

The Unknown To Expert 5 Star System illuminates your path to success. But this path is ongoing.

I have been developing the profile of experts and thought leaders for over 20 years, and I know that the story has no end. The story continues, because you don't stop here.

You continue to find opportunities to share your opinions, to teach people about your topic. You blog, tweet, you get up on stage and tell the world what you do.

I still constantly revisit parts of the Unknown To Expert 5 Star System. I redo my bio, edit speaking topics, pitch myself to journalists and consistently maintain my profile.

I still find that I have to overcome challenging spotlight moments.

I find live TV scary! I get asked to go on a business channel which is live and each time I get asked to be an expert panellist I want to throw up from nerves! I go back to the Catriona on 9 November 2010 who found it so challenging to step into the spotlight but did it anyway.

When I'm in this situation I think of you. I think about how my expertise and knowledge is real. It's earned. And it needs to be shared because I have something to say.

I know that the Unknown To Expert 5 Star System is a pathway that moves you from darkness to a star that people see. They take notice of you. You are illuminated.

Now your star is bright. You are truly a known expert.

I look forward to you continuing to make the world a better place by sharing your ideas, opinions and expertise as a recognised expert and thought leader.

Check out **www.UnknownToExpert.com**
for all of the action steps. Read the inspiring blog
about moving from Unknown To Expert.

Get inspired with Catriona Pollard

Catriona is passionate about social media, public relations, business and bringing them all together to create real, financial success for entrepreneurs and organisations.

Catriona can speak with authority on a range of topics that appeal to both entrepreneurs and corporates. She shares the challenges she has faced moving from unknown to expert, practical social media and PR tactics for businesses and so much more.

Catriona is renowned for being an inspiring presenter that shares practical skills and expertise so attendees can immediately implement what they've learnt to see real results.

She has shared her dynamic and practical expertise with thousands of people – who all leave energised, inspired and ready to take action.

Catriona is particularly passionate about women in leadership and has delivered presentations to thousands of women leaders about how to use communication in leadership to build careers and businesses.

Catriona Pollard is the founder and director of CP Communications—one of Australia's most respected and innovative PR and social media agencies.

Catriona is a highly regarded expert and media commentator in PR and social media and her views on social media and PR have been extensively published in media.

If you are looking for a passionate keynote or practical workshop please contact:

CP Communications

Suite 404, 10-12 Clarke Street, Crows Nest

+61 2 9460 9200, info@cpcommunications.com.au

W: www.cpcommunications.com.au

L: au.linkedin.com/in/catrionapollard

Y: www.youtube.com/user/PublicRelationsTips

Made in the USA
San Bernardino, CA
16 May 2014